THE HOLY MUSHROOM
Evidence of Mushrooms in
Judeo-Christianity

A critical re-evaluation of the schism between John M. Allegro
and R. Gordon Wasson over the theory on the entheogenic origins
of Christianity presented in *The Sacred Mushroom and the Cross*

By

J. R. Irvin
with Jack Herer

[signature] 3/1/2010

Published 2008
Gnostic Media
Research & Publishing
www.gnosticmedia.com

THE HOLY MUSHROOM:

Evidence of Mushrooms in Judeo-Christianity

A critical re-evaluation of the schism between John M. Allegro and R. Gordon Wasson over the theory on the entheogenic origins of Christianity presented in The Sacred Mushroom and the Cross

© 2008 J. R. Irvin

ISBN 10: 0982556209
ISBN 13: 9780982556207
Library of Congress Control Number: 2008909509

1st printing October 2008, 2nd printing September 2009

Table of Contents

Acknowledgements vi

Foreword ix

Preface xiii

Introduction 1

The Wasson and Allegro missives 8

    1) Wasson to TLS, pub. 21 August 1970 8

        Commentary 9

    2) Allegro to TLS, written 31 August, pub. 11 September 1970 12

        Commentary 12

    3) Wasson's private letter to Allegro, 14 September 1970 14

        Commentary 15

    4) Wasson to Arthur Crook, Ed., TLS, 16 September 1970 17

        Commentary 18

    5) Wasson to TLS, written 16 September, pub. 25 September 1970 19

        Commentary 23

Allegro's References and Citations 31

    Citations to Professor John Ramsbottom 32

    Citations to R. Gordon Wasson 48

    Citations to Robert Graves 59

    Citations to Dr. S. Henry Wassen 66

    Citations to Dr. Andrija Puharich 68

    Citations to Dr. Richard Evans Schultes 74

Other Unsupported Claims 79

Additional evidence of Mushrooms in Judeo-Christianity 107

The Epistle to the Renegade Bishops 149

    Judaism and Islam 150

Conclusion 154

Appendix—The Allegro-Wasson Controversy 161

References 165

Index 171

Acknowledgements

Special thanks to Judith Anne Brown and Anna Partington, without whose help this project would have been impossible. Also thanks to Jack Herer, Professor Carl A. P. Ruck at Boston University, Professor John Rush at Sierra College, Professor Neil Whitehead at the University of Wisconsin, Professor Benny Shanon at Hebrew University of Jerusalem (Israel), Dr. Brian Akers, Greg Hardesty, Richard Andrew Grove and Lisa Arbercheski, Edward Milhuisen, Peter Webster, Edzard Klapp, Michael Hoffman, Jonathan Ott, Bartlomiej Walczak, Kris Millegan and Martin Lee for their invaluable contributions and/or feedback. Thanks to John W. Allen for his *Psilocybe* images; and also thanks to Mark Hoffman for some of the Christian iconography images, and for kindly providing a much-needed research copy of *Entheos* Vol. 1 No. 2.

Condemnation without investigation is the height of ignorance.
~ Albert Einstein

Foreword

Why should we be surprised or shocked by the idea that people of all eras and cultures have used hallucinatory drugs to attain exalted states of consciousness, which they take to mean divine understanding? In *The Sacred Mushroom and the Cross* John Allegro tried to show that this idea was built into the language and thought of religion from the very earliest times, and was still evident in the language and thought of the first Christians.

When survival depended on the fertility of the earth, and fertility was a gift of the gods, people sought to promote fertility by appealing to divine power. The swiftest and surest way to know the mind of god was through the use of herbal drugs. Throughout all ages and across all continents, priests and shamans have used entheogenic drugs in religious rituals. One of the chief sources of these drugs was fly agaric, *Amanita muscaria,* the sacred mushroom.

John Allegro believed that Judaism and Christianity were no exception. He held that many biblical stories and sayings derived from earlier fertility cults based on the use of the sacred mushroom. He discerned mushroom epithets behind many stories, names and phrases in the Old and New Testaments, either elaborated into folk tales or deliberately hidden in names and incantations. Embedded in different contexts, and often misunderstood in translation, they still carried messages for those who would look for them.

His evidence was linguistic. Starting with Greek and Semitic names, phrases, themes and stories from the Old and New Testaments, he followed them back through Phoenician and Akkadian to the earliest known writings – those of Sumer in the third millennium BCE. Although the precise form and interpretation of words changed with inflection and context in different languages, he found that the basic phonemes, the building blocks of words, carried their root meaning from one context to another. So by tracing the development of words we can trace the intertwining evolution of language, culture and religion.

The Sacred Mushroom and the Cross met outrage and derision. Part of the problem lay in common revulsion at the idea of linking Christianity to primitive fertility cults. The idea that the New Testament was a cover story, deliberately designed to transmit occult knowledge to a particular sect without the authorities realising it, seemed improbably complicated. Also, Allegro based his evidence almost entirely on language study, and not enough was known about Sumerian to make a solid case. Had he given more attention to investigating the surviving cultural and artistic expressions of 'Christian' fertility cults, he might have convinced more people of the strength of his argument.

But now other types of evidence are coming forward to show that elements of the ancient religion survived at least into medieval times, where they were widely accepted in pagan and Christian folklore and religious practice, if not openly condoned by the established Church. For example, a fresco in a thirteenth-century church at Plaincourault, France, shows *Amanita muscaria* as the Tree of Life. Allegro used it as an illustration to *The Sacred Mushroom and the Cross*, but in the outcry against the book even this obvious reference to mushroom veneration met denial.

Starting with the Plaincourault fresco, Jan Irvin sets out to justify John Allegro's stance and to explore the objections to it. As I explained in the biography *John Marco Allegro: The Maverick of the Dead Sea Scrolls*, the main doubts about Allegro's theory are whether the New Testament could deliberately conceal a secret code about mushroom usage, and the need to further substantiate Sumerian word connections. In the light of Irvin's findings, there can now be little doubt that entheogenic drugs were used to attain divine understanding in Christianity as in other religions. I also think it is worth questioning whether mushroom lore was as secret as Allegro assumed it to be: lost in translation, perhaps, but not lost on the early followers of the cult, for whom the symbolism of the holy mushroom was a guide to revelation. In this book Jan Irvin subjects both sides to courtroom-like scrutiny, and adds powerful new evidence to help fill the gaps in our understanding of the origins of religion.

~ Judith Anne Brown
Author of *John Marco Allegro: The Maverick of the Dead Sea Scrolls*

Preface

Beginning in the 1950s a serious theoretical disagreement regarding art interpretations emerged within the fields of theology and entheobotany. Entheobotany is the study of how certain cultures use plants and fungi for religious purposes. The question at the heart of this disagreement concerns the study of the origins of religion, and more specifically Judeo-Christianity. Gaining an insight into the core issues of this disagreement is of utmost importance to anyone with an interest in understanding the origins of religion.

The question: Were psychoactive drugs involved in the foundation of Christianity?

This question has caused a schism within theological studies, and especially within the field of entheobotany itself.

One side argues that the use of psychoactive substances can be traced only up until, and their impact is limited to, the earliest writings of Genesis, about 1000_{BCE}—which excludes Christianity.

The other side argues that the use of psychoactive substances was more widespread and persistent. It has been central to the foundation of nearly all religion, including Christianity, and evidence of this usage can be found into more modern times.

It is important for biblical theologians and entheobotany scholars alike to understand the cause and effect of this schism if open dialogue is to continue. Until this issue is resolved and faced head on, scholarship, in regard to Judeo-Christianity, is at a standstill.

Introduction

In 1952 a leading art historian, Dr. Erwin Panofsky, wrote to a famed amateur mycologist, R. Gordon Wasson, that the Plaincourault fresco depicting a mushroom tree with Adam and Eve (see Plate 1) was not of a mushroom, but a stylized Italian pine tree. Wasson adopted Panofsky's interpretation and thenceforth began to force it upon other scholars. Uncritical acceptance of the Wasson-Panofsky view lasted, unchecked, for nearly fifty years. However, a more questioning approach reveals that their interpretation of the Plaincourault fresco mushroom has caused a major and unnecessary schism in biblical theology and entheobotany. Recently Michael Hoffman and I reevaluated the critical points of the 'Plaincourault as Pine' argument in *Wasson and Allegro on the Tree of Knowledge as Amanita* (Hoffman et al, 2006). Other scholars, including Professor Carl Ruck and Giorgio Samorini, have also recently attacked the Wasson-Panofsky interpretation (Ruck et al, 2007/2005/2001/ unpublished; Samorini, 1998).

The purpose of the following study is to show the source of the schism between two primary opposing theories within the field of entheobotany, as well as these theories' lasting effects on biblical scholarship. The theories are as follows:

1) Psychoactive substances, and especially mushrooms, were used only at the earliest stages of the formation of Judeo-Christianity. Their usage does not go beyond circa 1000_{BCE}. It was possibly reflected in the writing of the Book of Genesis and the story of Adam and Eve and may extend into other minor heretical Christian sects. There is no evidence that psychoactive substances were used in the foundation or body of Christianity itself. Depictions of these substances in art work, such as the Plaincourault fresco, are purely fortuitous misinterpretations.

This theory was first advanced by R. Gordon Wasson, the

famous amateur mycologist who in *Soma, Divine Mushroom of Immortality*, 1968, proposed that the Rig Vedic Soma was the *Amanita muscaria* mushroom – a theory widely accepted today.

2) Psychoactive substances, and especially mushrooms, were not only a factor in the earliest stages of the formation of Judaism, but a core part of Christianity's foundations. Their usage may be seen to extend into more modern times. This fact is evidenced by, but not limited to, artwork such as the Plaincourault fresco.

This theory was first advanced by John M. Allegro, the famous Dead Sea Scrolls scholar and University of Manchester philologist, who proposed in *The Sacred Mushroom and the Cross*, 1970, that Christianity was based on a fertility drug cult. This proposal destroyed his career.

Supporters of either of these theories have briefly and sporadically argued their points of view in various writings on entheogens for nearly four decades—more often than not, rather uncritically.

The theories do not affect only the field of entheobotany, but have had strong and lasting implications for theology as a whole, especially with regard to biblical scholarship and the study of the origins of Judeo-Christianity.

Scholars who have been swept up into this schism include, but are certainly not limited to:

- Dr. John Pilch, Dr. Dan Merkur and Jonathan Ott, who have clearly stated their positions against Allegro;
- Dr. Andy Letcher, who has written an entire book maintaining that the religious use of mushrooms is strictly a modern phenomena (herein disproved)—attacking both Wasson *and* Allegro (Letcher, 2007);

- Professor Carl Ruck and Professor John Rush who have written in support of many of Allegro's ideas;
- D.M. Murdock (Acharya S.), who supports some of Allegro's ideas (Acharya S., 1999); and
- Dr. Robert Price, who at one point sided with Wasson, but has since accepted some of Allegro's ideas.

In Price's original review of Acharya's book *The Christ Conspiracy*, he wrote:

> Having mentioned the Dionysian associations of the hallucinogenic mushroom, it behooves me to mention [Acharya's] rehash of John Allegro's claim (in *The Sacred Mushroom and the Cross*) that an ancient Christian catacomb fresco depicts Adam and Eve flanking, not a tree, but a red-capped *Amanita muscaria* mushroom, implying perhaps that the early Christians cherished the forbidden knowledge of the mushroom, as the ancient Soma priests of India did.
>
> [Acharya] likes this, as a bit of New Age pot-smoking apologetics. But, unfortunately for this theory, art historian Erwin Panofsky declares that "the plant in this fresco has nothing whatever to do with mushrooms... and the similarity with Amanita muscaria is purely fortuitous. The Plaincourault fresco is only one example – and, since the style is provincial, a particularly deceptive one – of a conventionalized tree type, prevalent in Romanesque and early Gothic art, which art historians actually refer to as a 'mushroom tree'... It comes about by the gradual schematization of the impressionistically rendered Italian pine tree in Roman and early Christian painting, and there are hundreds of instances exemplifying this development... the medieval artists hardly ever worked from nature but from classical prototypes which in the course of repeated copying became quite unrecognizable" (quoted in Wendy Doniger O'Flaherty, "The Post-Vedic History of the Soma

Plant," in R. Gordon Wasson (ed.) Soma: Divine Mushroom of
Immortality. pp. 179–180).

~ Robert Price, review of *The Christ Conspiracy*

Price has since removed his entire review of Acharya's book from
his website and replaced it with a promise for a revision.
(http://www.robertmprice.mindvendor.com/rev_murdock.htm)

Understanding this schism is important because each time the topic
of psychoactive substances (entheogens) in Christianity is discussed,
Allegro's name is brought up in opposing arguments as if he is some
sort of joke, a show-stopper, the end-all to a logical discussion. As Pilch
wrote me personally:

> [W]e discussed Allegro when I was in graduate school in the
> late 1960's. His scholarship is not respected and his conclusions
> are fanciful. He should really write science fiction.
> ~ Dr. John Pilch, biblical scholar, Georgetown University

Wasson is perceived as credible in comparison with Allegro. But
Wasson doesn't cover entheogens in Christianity: Allegro does. Thus,
this anti-Allegro and pro-Wasson impression gives the appearance that
the theory of entheogens in Christianity is baseless.

The extent that Wasson covers *Amanita* in Judeo-Christianity is to
affirm its use in Genesis but reject it in Ezekiel, Revelation and later
Christian practice. But Allegro finds entheogens in the entire Bible era,
and to some extent after, as in the Plaincourault fresco.

To overly credit Wasson and under-credit Allegro is to underestimate
the extent of entheogen use throughout the Bible era and later. It is to
give all credit to Wasson in an unbalanced way.

Wasson's theory is preventing Allegro's paradigm-changing research from being applied to the field of Christian origins—thus preventing the evolution of this field of study and causing its stagnation.

Not recognizing Wasson's flaws is preventing Allegro's voice from being heard and his valid contributions from being recognized and integrated into these fields. As long as Wasson is seen as irreproachable he is preventing scholars from recognizing the value of Allegro's insights.

When it comes to many of the arguments against Allegro, misconstruing and manufacturing evidence where often none exists seems to be standard protocol. Allegro's ideas, and the ideas of those that have continued this area of research, are often swept aside without justification. They are too often dismissed and ignored in an uncritical and largely unfounded diatribe which refuses to review the specific points of the arguments:

- Does the Plaincourault fresco really represent mushrooms?
- Were Christian origins based in fertility cults and drug use?
- Were entheogens used in Christianity, even to modern times?

This study helps to reveal the errors in claims such as these:

- The Plaincourault fresco does not represent a mushroom—art historians say so having studied the matter.
- Entheogen use is limited to pre-Christian times and fringe heretical sects.
- Allegro was on the lunatic fringe, a crazy man, out for scholarly revenge. His research is utterly unfounded.
- Allegro took most of his ideas from Wasson.
- Wasson later changed his position to support for Allegro's work and the idea of mushrooms in Judeo-Christianity.

Included herein is a complete list and analysis of Allegro's entheobotanical citations used in *The Sacred Mushroom and the Cross*

(SMC). These citations are intentionally limited to those with specific regard to entheogens. The analysis includes important textual references which set out the arguments used for and against both Wasson and Allegro.

These references also reveal errors Allegro copied from other scholars, as well as several of his own errors. All of these errors are extremely important to the discussion herein. When we review the citations in a structured format, it is beyond reasonable doubt that Allegro took the blame for many errors that were not his own but those he simply copied from other scholars. This happens especially with regard to the chemical constituents, taste and effects of the fly-agaric, *Amanita muscaria*. The original errors, and the scholars who made them, were largely, if not completely, ignored.

In order to give the reader the best possible understanding of this schism, both the personal letters and the letters published in *The Times Literary Supplement* (*TLS*) between Wasson and Allegro are included in full. Also included and analyzed is a significant letter from Wasson to the editor of the *TLS*, Arthur Crook. These letters are provided in full because they form the foundation of this study and reveal the origins of the schism between Wasson and Allegro. In doing so, they also reveal the beginnings of the schism in the field of entheobotany, and beyond into Judeo-Christian theology, which has continued to the present day.

Critical analysis of the words exchanged between Wasson and Allegro suggests a deeper, almost hidden, argument between the two men. I suggest this argument has caused serious shockwaves that have had strong, long-lasting repercussions on theological research, especially with regard to Judeo-Christian origins, long after both their deaths.

For example, Allegro caught Wasson in contradiction of himself. Wasson consequently appears angry toward Allegro, lashing out at him in the press, personal letters, and interviews. And to the undiscerning public eye, Wasson's antipathy appears justified. Allegro's point ends up being almost completely overlooked, and from there he remains unresponsive, which appears to only further escalate the antipathy of Wasson, who continues his attacks almost until his death, sixteen years later.

Commentary throughout this study analyses the critical points.

The Wasson and Allegro missives

1) Wasson to TLS, pub. 21 August 1970

Sir, I have just read John M. Allegro's *The Sacred Mushroom and the Cross* (reviewed in the TLS on May 28). I will refrain from passing on his philological evidence, which others have already treated thoroughly. But I will call your readers' attention to a question of art history, that I have not seen mentioned in the various reviews that have come to my attention.

Facing page 74 of his book Mr Allegro exhibits a photograph of what he calls "a Christian fresco showing the *Amanita muscaria* as the tree of good and evil in the Garden of Eden". His publishers have reproduced a mirror-image of this on each of the end-papers of the book and also on the jacket.

This fresco, an expression of French provincial Romanesque art, was first called to the attention of the learned world in the Bulletin of the *Société Mycologique de France* in 1911 (vol. xxvii, p. 31). It has been picked up frequently in mycological publications, especially in England. Mycologists speak only to each other and never to art historians. Had they done so, the story would have been different.

I drew attention to this error in our *Mushrooms, Russia & History* (1957) and at greater length in my *SOMA Divine Mushroom of Immortality* (1969). In this last book I quoted from a letter that Erwin Panofsky had written me in 1952:

The plant in this fresco has nothing whatever to do with mushrooms... and the similarity with Amanita muscaria is purely fortuitous. The Plaincourault fresco is only one example – and since the style is provincial, a particularly deceptive one

– of a conventionalized tree type, prevalent in Romanesque and early Gothic art, which art historians actually refer to as a "mushroom tree", or in German, Pilzbaum. It comes about by the gradual schematization of the impressionistically rendered Italian pine tree in Roman and early Christian painting, and there are hundreds of instances exemplifying this development – unknown of course to mycologists. [...] What the mycologists have overlooked is that the medieval artists hardly ever worked from nature but from classical prototypes which in the course of repeated copying became quite unrecognizable.

I checked with other art historians including Meyer Schapiro, and found that they were in agreement. I was struck by the celerity with which they all recognized the art motif.

One could expect mycologists, in their isolation, to make this blunder. Mr Allegro is not a mycologist but, if anything, a cultural historian. On page 229 of his book, in his notes, he shows himself familiar with my writings. Presumably he had read the footnote in which I dismissed the fresco on page 87 of *Mushrooms, Russia & History* and, more especially, Panofsky's letter reproduced on page 179 of *SOMA*. He chooses to ignore the interpretation put on this fresco by the most eminent art historians.

R. GORDON WASSON

Commentary
Unsolicited, Wasson fires his first attack against Allegro.

He states: "I drew attention to this error [Plaincourault fresco as mushroom] in our *Mushrooms, Russia & History* (1957) and at greater length in my *SOMA Divine Mushroom of Immortality* (1969)."

Buried in a footnote on page 87 of *Mushrooms, Russia and History*, we find:

> The Bulletin of the Société Mycologique de France in 1911 (vol. xxvii. P. 31) announced to the mycological world the discovery of a 13th century fresco representing the temptation of Eve. The mycologists who focused their attention on this fresco persuaded themselves that the Tree of Good and Evil had been portrayed by the artist as an amanita muscaria. The fresco, which we visited in the summer of 1952, is in a disaffected chapel in France, in the Berry, between Ingrandes and Mérigny, near the Château de Plaincourault. The style is Romanesque, and this fits the date that the edifice bears – 1291. Since the initial announcement there have been numerous references to the fresco in mycological publications: e. g., *The Romance of the Fungus World*, by R.T. and F.W. Rolfe, London, 1925, p. 291; also John Ramsbottom's *Mushrooms & Toadstools*, pp. 40-7 and illustration facing p. 34; also *The Illustrated London News*, Nov. 21, 1953. The mycologists would have done well to consult art historians. The Plaincourault fresco does not represent a mushroom and has no place in a discussion of ethno-mycology. It is a typical stylized Palestinian tree, of the type familiar to students of Byzantine and Romanesque art. The German art historians have even devised for this oft-repeated motif the technical designation of *Pilzbaum*.
>
> ~ Gordon Wasson

Attacking Ramsbottom and the Rolfes et al, Wasson says: "The mycologists who focused their attention on this fresco persuaded themselves that the Tree of Good and Evil had been portrayed by the artist as an amanita muscaria". As plate 1 shows, the Plaincourault fresco does in fact clearly portray a hybridized *A. muscaria* mushroom, as several scholars have since shown (Hoffman et al, 2006; Ruck et al, 2007/2005/2001/unpublished; Samorini, 1998). Wasson next states that the chapel is "disaffected," which can have various meanings, such as: evilly affected, unfriendly, hostile, disliked, regarded with aversion—or simply alienated or unused. But he seems to choose this word to create the illusion of separation between the chapel and Christianity. He then says: "The mycologists would have done well to consult art historians." Never mind that art historians don't study mycology, which he later admits in *Soma* (pg. 179–80, below). He continues: "The Plaincourault fresco does not represent a mushroom and has no place in a discussion of ethno-mycology. It is a typical stylized Palestinian tree..." This, however, contradicts (or predates) Wasson's letter (above) where he states that the mushroom tree is an "impressionistically rendered Italian pine tree".

But Wasson also avoids admitting that in *Soma* (pg. 221) he says the Plaincourault fresco does, nonetheless, *indirectly* represent the mushroom:

> [...] the mycologists were right also, in a transcendental sense of which neither they nor the artist had an inkling, when they saw a serpent offering a mushroom to Eve in the Fresco of Plaincourault.
> ~ Gordon Wasson

These contradictions will be key points throughout the rest of this study.

In the last paragraph of his letter, Wasson makes an unnecessary jab at Allegro. Wasson states: "Mr Allegro is not a mycologist but, if anything, a cultural historian." Wasson doesn't just say Allegro is not a mycologist, the likes of which he's just put down, but includes the caveat "if anything," purely as an insult to Allegro. Wasson was himself a banker and not a professional mycologist or art historian. Allegro, contrary to the image that Wasson wants to portray of him, was an eminent cultural historian, theologian, and philologist. It's true that he wasn't a mycologist—but then Wasson has just criticized the mycologists for not studying art.

2) Allegro to TLS, written 31 August, pub. 11 September 1970

Sir, Is it too much to hope that persons who presume to comment critically on my book, The *Sacred Mushroom and the Cross*, would read it thoroughly first? Mr Gordon Wasson's (August 21) objections to the mycologists' identification of the Plaincourault fresco's tree of good and evil as the Amanita muscaria are quoted verbatim in n. 20 to chapter IX.

One other point: "others" have not, in fact, "treated thoroughly" my philological evidence for the identification of the mushroom cult and mythology in the ancient Near East adequately to assess the results of this major advance in language relationships, now presented for the first time in published form, will require much longer unemotional study by competent philologists than has yet been possible. Until this has been done, laymen would be well advised to ignore the kind of emotive criticism of my work so far expressed by clerical and other reviewers and read the whole book for themselves.

JOHN M. ALLEGRO

Commentary

Allegro fired back at Wasson for not having read the book before writing his critical commentary. And though Wasson claims to have read Allegro's book in his August 21 letter to the *TLS*, it appears most likely that he only gave the book a superficial and second-hand evaluation. Jack Herer, author of *The Emperor Wears No Clothes,* has recounted to me on several occasions his telephone conversation with Wasson in

February 1984. Herer had just spent six months examining many of Allegro's references. He called Wasson to ask him personally why he felt Allegro's work was incorrect. As Herer recalls the conversation, Wasson informed him that he had actually been too busy to read Allegro's book, and that two respected friends, a Jewish Rabbi and a Catholic Monsignor, reviewed it and reported back to him that "there was not one single word of truth in the book whatsoever." (See the Appendix for a full transcript of Herer's conversation with Wasson.) In conversations and emails, Ruck confirmed Herer's statements.

Allegro goes on to reference chapter IX, footnote 20. Footnote 20 is a contradictory statement by Wasson. In *SMC*, chapter 9, Allegro describes the fresco as recalling the tradition of the Eden story as mushroom-based mythology: "Even as late as the thirteenth century some recollection of the old tradition was known among Christians, to judge from a fresco painted on the wall of a ruined church in Plaincourault in France (pl. 2). There the *Amanita muscaria* is gloriously portrayed, entwined with a serpent, while Eve stands by holding her belly." Allegro continues in note 20 to this chapter: "Despite rejection of identity of the subject ('rightly or wrongly') as being a mushroom by R. Gordon Wasson: 'for almost a half-century mycologists have been under a misapprehension on this matter' (qu. Ramsbottom *op. cit.* p. 48)".

Allegro had found this quote from Wasson—that "rightly or wrongly, for almost a half-century mycologists have been under a misapprehension on this matter"—printed in a second edition of Ramsbottom's book *Mushrooms & Toadstools,* pg. 48. Ramsbottom had taken it from a private letter that Wasson had written to him dated December 21, 1953, regarding the Plaincourault fresco and the Panofsky interpretation. As is shown below, Wasson was unaware at this stage that his private letter had been printed sixteen years earlier in the second edition of Ramsbottom's book, which Allegro used. From a purely intellectual perspective, Allegro had beaten Wasson by using his own words against him. But unfortunately, the rebuttal, while technically complete, is too vague for public reading. The proper response from Allegro would have been to reprint Wasson's entire letter to Ramsbottom in the *TLS*, with full commentary. If Allegro had done so, his own reputation would have been strengthened, and Wasson's reputation weakened. Instead, Allegro published his short and dismissive response. Academia and the public at large missed Allegro's point, but Wasson didn't. Wasson was furious.

3) Wasson's private letter to Allegro, 14 September 1970

Dear Mr Allegro

At last I understand. From your letter in the TLS 11.9.70 I surmise what had baffled me. I had found your note IX 20 incomprehensible. In nothing that I had published had I used the words apparently attributed to me, and it wasn't 100% clear whether you were attributing them to me or to Ramsbottom. I looked up 'Ramsbottom op. cit. p. 48' and I found nothing there. In the fall of 1953 as I passed through London I saw an ad of Collins announcing a new book on mushrooms by Ramsbottom. (The date was the day it was put on sale, October 26.) I bought it and hurried home. On December 21 I wrote a letter to Dr. Ramsbottom pointing out the misinterpretation of the Plaincourault fresco in his book on page 34. I now gather that he was properly impressed and added a footnote, not to be found in the original edition, on p. 48. He never replied to my letter (which is not unusual with him), and he neither sought nor had my permission to reproduce what was a private letter. The letter was not drafted for publication. I had forgotten its text, which I have now looked up for the first time since it was written, and find the words you quote in it. What we wished to say we said in *Mushrooms, Russia & History* (1957) and I added

Panofsky's letter in my *SOMA*. Does your copy of *Mushrooms and Toadstools* carry '1953' on its title page? If so, it is misleading, because it was either a fresh print or a new edition published at the earliest in 1954.

Though we are utterly opposed to each other on the role played by the fly-agaric, we agree that it was important. I think we can correspond with each other on friendly terms, like opposing counsel after hammering each other all day in court who meet for a drink together in a bar before going home. I wish you would tell me one thing: when did the idea of the fly-agaric first come to you and from where?

Sincerely yours,

R. Gordon Wasson

Commentary

Wasson first says he couldn't find the reference to which Allegro was referring him in Ramsbottom's book (below). This is because Allegro confused the first edition, published in October 1953, with the second edition, published four months later in January 1954. Wasson continues with a story about how he first discovered Ramsbottom's book in London on the very day it was released, October 26, 1953. He mentions how on December 21, one month before the second edition of Ramsbottom's book was printed, he sent Ramsbottom a letter which he, being "properly impressed," included in the second edition.

Wasson then discusses how Ramsbottom didn't respond, which he suggests "is not unusual with him", and how he did not ask permission to reprint the letter. Wasson mentions that it was a private letter, "not drafted for publication." He then states, or backpedals, that what he wished to say, or tell the public, he said in his 1957 publication (above).

However, this implies that Wasson actually believes two things: those that are private, and those that he published, which I'll discuss more later. Wasson goes on to mention Allegro's error regarding the first and second editions of Ramsbottom's book.

Let's take another angle. Here we see Wasson attempting to influence the leading respected authority on mushrooms, Ramsbottom, about the interpretation of the Plaincourault fresco. Ramsbottom takes Wasson's entire letter, faults and all, and prints it in the second edition of his book, pg. 48. He doesn't even bother to reply to Wasson to let him know that his letter was published. Ramsbottom is likely thinking: "OK, Wasson, have it your way. Who is the reader going to side with: me, with a simple natural interpretation (Plaincourault fresco looks like *Amanita*, and represents it), or Wasson who says that 'rightly or wrongly', he's going to reject it as *Amanita*, based on the authority of art scholars who don't study mushrooms?"

Wasson doesn't figure out what Ramsbottom did to him until sixteen years later, in 1970, when Allegro found the letter and not only published a reference to it in his own book, but shed daylight upon it in the *TLS*. Once Wasson figures out what Ramsbottom did with his letter, he objects to his own waffling yet authoritarian position being highlighted in the pages of Ramsbottom's book, and in the *TLS*. We then see Wasson backpedaling to Allegro regarding his own words written to Ramsbottom, as if to say to Ramsbottom: "Hey, I didn't intend for you to actually print in your book what I professed and wrote you about!"

This scenario is most intriguing. Wasson writes to a famous authority he's trying to influence, who then elevates his letter – inconsistencies and all – fully into his book. Realizing it sixteen years later, Wasson objects to its publication. It's the backpedaling of Wasson that arrests our attention: You've got to say X! Hey, I didn't mean for you to print my letter that says "You've got to say X!"

But Wasson still fails to realize how he's been had. Not only was his letter given the compliment, or ignominy, of being included as a "footnote", but Ramsbottom put Wasson's letter in the very body of his text as an "Addendum". This just happens to be the perfect place for someone like Allegro to find it.

I propose that Allegro was pointing out Wasson's doubts when he briefly quoted Wasson's words "rightly or wrongly". He was letting Wasson's indecision speak for itself. This is how Ramsbottom and Allegro saw, and intended to portray, Wasson's letter denying the depiction of *Amanita* in the Plaincourault fresco – they revealed Wasson's position as incongruous and tenuous.

The last paragraph, which will be further discussed later, is interesting. Wasson knows that Allegro has gotten the better of him. Attempting to be affable, and perhaps cover up the seriousness of their differences, he therefore suggests that they correspond: "on friendly terms, like opposing counsel after hammering each other all day in court who meet for a drink together in a bar before going home." Maybe Wasson himself felt "hammered" on.

Wasson sent the above private letter on September 14, two days before he wrote his public letter of September 16 to the *TLS* (see (5) below), published on September 25, 1970, thus not allowing Allegro adequate response time. Wasson omitted the core facts of both his private missives to Allegro and Ramsbottom in the public letter.

With the letter to the *TLS*, Wasson sent a cover note to the editor:

4) Wasson to Arthur Crook, Ed., TLS, 16 September 1970

I think Allegro must have got his idea of the fly-agaric from us, yet his book does not show any influence by us, apart from the fly-agaric.

~ R. Gordon Wasson

Commentary

The general reader and public at large miss Allegro's point. Allegro rejected Wasson with his own words, publicly revealing Wasson's contradictory position as feeble. So why then did Wasson write another self-contradictory letter to Crook, editor of the *TLS*? If not for purely strategic reasons, then what was the point of his writing this letter to the editor? Looking at the correspondences overall, we can logically surmise that Wasson was seeking to influence the opinion of the *TLS* on his behalf, even though Allegro had already technically debunked Wasson by using his own waffling words to Ramsbottom, "rightly or wrongly," against him.

It is important to recognize Wasson's statement to Crook as completely contradictory. Either Allegro was influenced by Wasson, or he wasn't. Furthermore, we must question the very statement Wasson made to Crook. Is Wasson attempting to imply that Allegro took the idea from his *Mushrooms, Russia and History*, 1957, or from *Soma, Divine Mushroom of Immortality*, 1968? The reason this question is of utmost importance is because, as we know from popular press articles regarding Allegro, he went public with the idea of the drug origins of Christianity on or before Friday, October 13, 1967:

> Scrolls Scholar Slaps At Biblical Cornerstones
> By Godfrey Anderson
>
> LONDON (AP) — A Hebrew language scholar unraveling the Dead Sea Scrolls suggested Friday that Christianity's roots lay in a drug-taking cult and that the New Testament was "just a cover story" for it.
> He said the Old Testament prophets, when they saw visions, were probably "taking a trip" on LSD or something like it.

John Marco Allegro, lecturer on Old Testament and intertestamental studies at Manchester University [...]
~ The Fresno Bee, October 14, 1967

The story was also reported the same day in similar terms in several other newspapers, including:

- *Galveston Daily*
- *Daily Oklahoman*
- *The News*
- *Times-Mirror and Observer*
- *The Winnipeg Free Press.*

This would make any contention by Wasson that Allegro took the theory from *Soma, Divine Mushroom of Immortality,* incredible.

It will become evident that the reason "...his book does not show any influence by us..." is simply because Wasson was not a major source for Allegro's research.

5) Wasson to TLS, written 16 September, pub. 25 September 1970

The Sacred Mushroom

Sir,-Mr. Allegro (September 11) chooses to avoid the point of my letter: the Plaincourault fresco does *not* picture the fly-agaric. He admits, even insists, that he had been forewarned, but none the less for guidance on a question of medieval iconography he has stuck to a naive misinterpretation made by a band of eager mycologists, and only because he thinks this would serve his thesis. Some would have preferred the judgment of specialists in Romanesque art.

Mr. Allegro's uncritical choice of sources is again made manifest on page 123 of his book, where he takes up the chemistry of the fly-agaric. "Among the drugs so far isolated", he says, "are Muscarine, Atropine, and Bufotenin." He cites as his authority a book published in 1959 by a man, not a chemist, who was at the time exploring E.S.P. and talking with the dead, especially with an Egyptian priest belonging to the family of a 4th Dynasty Pharaoh. Muscarine is found consistently in the fly-agaric but in quantities so small that one would have to ingest upwards of six kilos to get a muscarine reaction, and moreover this would not be hallucinogenic. Atropine has been reported, but several careful studies in recent years have failed to find it in American and European specimens and its very presence is now considered doubtful. As for Bufotenin, there is none in the fly-agaric.

In the past ten years chemists have done much to clarify the intricate problems presented by the fly-agaric, notably the Bowden team in England, the Takemoto team of Sendai University, and most important the team headed by Professor Conrad Eugster in Zürich. Mr. Allegro seems ignorant to their writings. The active agents are ibotenic acid, muscimol, and muscazone, but the fascinating problem of the fly-agaric is not yet fully solved and there may be other agents yet to be discovered. A recapitulation of the work in this field will appear in the October issue of the *Bulletin on Narcotics* published in Geneva by the Division of Narcotic Drugs of the United Nations.

May I ask the hospitality of your columns to clarify the difference that separates Mr. Allegro and me? We both think the role of the fly-agaric was of major importance in Eurasian cultural history. In the 1920s my wife and I began to interest ourselves in the widely varying attitudes toward wild mushrooms of the European peoples. For more than two decades we gathered data

– philological, folkloric, anthropological – on this theme, and these [caused] us, in the 1940s, to hazard a weak surmise: that a mushroom (we knew not which) had played a role in the religious life of our remote ancestors millennia ago, long before there was writing. Seeking light, we turned to the Asiatic cultures, and there we found two shrinking enclaves, in the remotest regions of the far north, where the shamans still made use of the fly-agaric as the hallucinogenic agent for communicating with the spirits of the dead. This seemed a gratifying confirmation of our surmise and we thought we had reached the end of our road. Our book, *Mushrooms Russia & History*, appeared in 1957.

In the 1960s I directed my attention to the Soma of the ancient Aryans, an hallucinogenic plant that saturates the Vedic hymns and that had never been identified. The descriptive terms of the poets, all of their varied tropes for the adored plant, tallied perfectly with the fly-agaric. No one had ever suggested a mushroom. The art and folklore of the Near and Middle East in the third and second millennium B.C. are saturated with a Marvellous Herb linked with a Tree of Life. They are, I contend, the fly-agaric and the tree with which it prefers to live in mycorrhizal relationship, the birch of the forest belt of Eurasia. Among the peoples of the Near and Middle East many hailed originally from the north and the brought down with them the tradition of the Tree and the Herb. The Semites absorbed the tradition at Mari and elsewhere. How much the peoples of the Near and Middle East knew of the plant, whether the memory of the potent herb was reinforced by supplies to esoteric circles coming from areas where the fly-agaric grows in quantity, I do not know.

I published my findings in 1969, without fanfare, in *SOMA Divine Mushroom of Immortality*. Warned by scholar-friends that my book might pass unnoticed as coming from without the fold of accredited scholars, I gave my theme a full-dress presentation aiming my book primarily at Vedic scholars, supplying the best illustrations well reproduced, printed on fine paper by Giovanni Mardersteig of Verona, in a fine binding – in short, dressed in apparel befitting the holy herb that was its subject. This unfortunately raised the cost. I arranged to have sent out as gifts, almost a third of the limited edition, chiefly to Indo-Iranian scholars [damaged text] [?some] to anthropologists, and a few to [?others] The book was quickly sold [?We heard...] that a Bern bookseller [...?] is offering a f[ew c]opi[es ...] in price. The ... well received. You m... [?] commentary (April 30), drew attention to M. Lévi Strauss's remarkable article devoted to it in *L'Homme*. In reviews and private communications, many have accepted or lean to my identification. I am to lead off in a discussion of the subject at the forthcoming International Congress of Orientalists in Canberra.

My book brings the role of the fly-agaric in the Near and Middle East down to 1000 B.C. Mr. Allegro's performance brings it down from 1000 B.C. to the time of Christ. He does not disclose where he got the idea of the fly-agaric. I know no Sumerian, but I do remark that in an area of pioneering scholarship he tosses around Sumerian roots with an agility and a self-assurance not customary among philologists. When he occasionally touches on subjects with which I am familiar, as the Plaincourault fresco and the chemistry of the fly-agaric, he is, well, unimpressive.

The peoples of the Near and Middle East about whom Mr. Allegro is writing were among the most gifted and sophisticated that mankind has produced, and they have left us incomparable monuments of their culture. That they should have centred their religious life on a drug with the horrifying properties he describes on pages 163-164 of his book is unthinkable. Now that we are on the brink of learning the secrets of the great hallucinogen of history, the fly-agaric, it would be a reflection on our own intelligence were we to get off on the wrong foot. Mr. Allegro in this passage exhibits the complete syndrome of the invincible Anglo-Saxon mycophobe.

Commentary

Wasson lashes out at Allegro for supposedly ignoring his warning. He accuses Allegro of relying "none the less for guidance" and having "stuck to a naïve misinterpretation made by a band of eager mycologists... because he thinks this would serve his thesis". However, it is Wasson who appears to intentionally ignore his own waffling words quoted in *SMC* ch. IX, footnote 20. He firmly states his position that the Plaincourault fresco, which does clearly portray a mushroom, "does *not* picture the fly-agaric". I already touched on how Wasson failed to mention that his own contradictory position published in *Soma* is that the Plaincourault fresco *indirectly* represents a mushroom. But Wasson's own stance can also be interpreted as naïve and held "only because he thinks this would serve his thesis", which happens to be that mushroom usage was limited to circa 1000_{BCE} and the book of Genesis—which is an inaccurate date, as Genesis was likely written around 586_{BCE} (Rush, 2008). For Wasson to admit that the Plaincourault fresco *directly* represents mushrooms would mean that his own position against mushrooms in Christianity (below) is untenable.

As mentioned, Michael Hoffman and I have explored Wasson's attack on Allegro with regard to the Plaincourault fresco in *Wasson and Allegro on the Tree of Knowledge as Amanita* (Hoffman et al, 2006). This article points out Wasson's various contradictory positions on the use of entheogens in Christianity, as stated in his publications. It also shows Panofsky's view of the Plaincourault fresco to be weak and illogical, and how Wasson has contrived a highly implausible argument in favour of this view. Wasson states: "Mr. Allegro's uncritical choice of sources is again made manifest [...] He cites as his authority a book published in 1959 by a man, not a chemist, who was at the time exploring E.S.P. and talking with the dead, especially with an Egyptian priest belonging to the family of a 4th Dynasty Pharaoh." This statement is interesting simply because, as will be shown, Allegro took his idea of the mushroom almost entirely from the publications of scholars with whom Wasson himself had worked.

Wasson attacked Allegro for citing the work of Dr. Andrija Puharich, whom he simply calls "a man". He doesn't mention that Puharich was in fact a medical doctor who had worked with the US military and had left his post as Captain of the Army Chemical Center at Edgewood, Maryland in April 1955 (Levenda, 2005). It was only two months later in June 1955 that Wasson himself worked with Puharich, though they had already met in February of that same year (Puharich, 1959, below). It appears that Puharich was in charge of collecting psychoactive compounds for government research. There is strong evidence to suggest that Puharich was actually working with the MK-ULTRA program, US Army Intelligence and the CIA (Levenda, 2005). As if to simultaneously disparage and protect Puharich, Wasson avoided mentioning him by name, *insulting him only indirectly*. Wasson's intentional selection of the words "a man" made Puharich seem less a professional and more an amateur, a lunatic amateur at that. In order to achieve maximum impact from his statement, and to leave the reader with the impression that Puharich, or rather "a man", was a fringe lunatic, Wasson added the comment about Puharich's exploring E.S.P. and talking with the dead – especially an Egyptian priest. But Wasson himself agreed to attempt E.S.P. mushroom experiments for Puharich while he was in Mexico from June 30 to July 4, 1955. In fact, Wasson even invited Puharich along for the trip (Puharich, 1959, pg. 83–86, 90, 96, 101). Wasson took a hypocritical stance to attack Allegro for things perfectly applicable to himself.

Allegro had read Puharich's book and knew that Wasson agreed to partake in Puharich's E.S.P. experiments. From reading Puharich, and Wasson's invitation to him, it would appear that Wasson and Puharich were on good terms. Allegro said nothing regarding Wasson's once again contradictory and mistakenly conflated position.

Wasson goes on to correctly state: "In the past ten years chemists have done much to clarify the intricate problems presented by the fly-agaric [...] Mr Allegro seems ignorant to their writings."

But this is only partially valid. Wasson is correct to say that chemists had done much to clarify the problems of the fly-agaric. However, as will be shown, each of the publications that were cited by Allegro, including Wasson's, contradict one another. Allegro was most likely confused over the more recent *Amanita* chemistry research. On closer inspection of the publications regarding the fly-agaric's chemistry (below), it becomes difficult to draw a final conclusion.

Wasson then asks: "May I ask the hospitality of your columns to clarify the difference that separates Mr. Allegro and me?"

This question sets the stage. Wasson is preparing to differentiate his position from Allegro's by discussing his personal history and the elaborate publication of his book. He's doing this in order to give himself clout. Then, seizing the sales pitch opportunity, Wasson launches into a seemingly conceited and wordy four-paragraph description of himself and his work, detailing its extravagant publication. He fails to consider that Allegro, too, could have gone into great detail on his own background in theology and philology and the study of the Dead Sea Scrolls and Christian origins, though Allegro does no such thing.

Wasson continues: "My book brings the role of the fly-agaric in the Near and Middle East down to 1000 B.C. Mr. Allegro's performance brings it down from 1000 B.C. to the time of Christ."

This comment is intended to lead the reader to the conclusion that, *solely* because of the Wasson-Panofsky interpretation of the Plaincourault fresco, "Allegro's performance" is baseless. This is why Wasson refers to his own work as "my book," but refers to Allegro's as a "performance". But to agree with Wasson would require an uncritical acceptance of the Wasson-Panofsky interpretation, and the assumption that no contrary evidence exists (see Hoffman et al, 2006; Ruck et al, 2007/2005/2001; Samorini, 1998). This tactic also seeks to place Wasson's biblical mushrooms in the harmless era of 1000_{BCE}, where they could pose no question, nor threat, to Christian orthodoxy. It sparks no interest in, nor investigation of, Christian origins. It only serves to highjack and nullify any inquiry that goes later than 1000_{BCE}, and put down the inquirer—on the assumption that entheogens weren't used in Judeo-Christian practice post 1000_{BCE}.

These tactics are not the work of an unbiased, open-minded academic, but someone with ulterior, limiting motives; someone who seeks to gain status as the *only* authority. It is this unfounded stance by Wasson that has caused the schism. It is his assumptive, bull-headed dance of words that has enforced it in the eyes of other scholars to the present day.

Allegro, rather than side-step a direct investigation of modern religion as Wasson does, decides to take the issue head on and investigate mushroom usage into Christianity. Wasson is therefore correct in realizing the importance of mushroom usage in early religious practice, but illogical in applying the realization. He illogically, or mendaciously, considers Christianity out of bounds and attempts to constrain Allegro (and Ramsbottom, above) by presenting himself as the final authority.

Next Wasson states: "He does not disclose where he got the idea of the fly-agaric."

This comment takes the reader off course: as if it really mattered where Allegro learned about the *Amanita*. Unless there is contention of plagiarism or unoriginality, what would be the point of Wasson's statement? But Wasson has stated in his cover letter to the editor of the

TLS, "his book does not show any influence by us," so the point, whatever it may be, is mooted. Regardless, Wasson was not the first to suggest the possibility of *Amanita muscaria* in religion. Allegro could have first learned about the *Amanita* from Ramsbottom or Robert Graves, both British, who in the 1950s both published works about the mushroom's possible relationship to religion.

Next, Wasson enters into the famous Sumerian question: "I know no Sumerian, but I do remark that in an area of pioneering scholarship he tosses around Sumerian roots with an agility and a self-assurance not customary among philologists."

Wasson is correct to be critical of the Sumerian issue, in that many of Allegro's word connections were speculative. However, most Sumerian scholars have no understanding of fertility cults and entheogens, just as art historians don't read mycology books. In *Astrotheology & Shamanism* (Irvin et al, 2006, pg. 55), we cite Sumerian expert Anna Partington, who states:

> Most people come to the field of Sumerian studies with a background in several early Mideastern languages. Although John was of a previous generation, he was, in common with most Orientalists, perfectly well equipped to deal with cuneiform languages. He found comparative linguistic study especially interesting; but early in his career the finding of the scrolls by the Dead Sea led him to specialise in translation of these Hebrew and Aramaic documents.

> Unfortunately, the comparative philological work presented in *SMC* [*The Sacred Mushroom and the Cross*] uses a number of hypothetical Sumerian words not attested in texts. These are marked with an asterisk following philological convention. This is akin to proposing there is a word in the English language 'bellbat' because the individual words 'bell' and 'bat' are known

to exist separately. Then again words of different languages are gathered together without the type of argument which would be expected in order to demonstrate possible relationship.

~ Anna Partington

In *Fungus Redivivus*, Ruck states:

The basic objection is that Sumerian is apparently sui generis, a language unrelated to any other, and hence similar sounding words in Hebrew, Greek, and other ancient languages can have no significance. Also that Allegro often hypothesized words not actually extant in Sumerian; this latter objection is, however, the standard linguistic procedure, to recreate the necessary missing bridges. As for the former, it leaves out of account the fact that geographically proximate peoples borrow, pun, and assimilate words, especially in the case of imported rituals and a sacred vocabulary. Cults, moreover, are apt to spread through imported foreign leaders or priesthoods, continuing to conduct the rites, at least at first, in the magical-religious formulae of their native tongue, as, for example, with the importation of the religion of Cybele from Anatolia into Rome in the year 205 BCE, where she was served at first exclusively by her Oriental priesthood until the time of the Emperor Claudius. [...]

The truth of the matter is simply that the language tree or the families of languages are contaminated; and the criticism of Allegro's linguistics is based upon outmoded and simplistic assumptions about a still evolving discipline. The immense learning behind Allegro's notes and references to ancient sources is dismissed by his critics, who hastened to silence him forever for proposing an unseemly and overly sexual context for the Judeo-Christian religion, scandalously embedded in the Anatolian fertility traditions of drug-induced ecstatic communion with the deity, something not only prevalent in the area, but also the expectable shamanic experience of all ancient religions. As a brilliant demonstration of mythopoeia and mythical analysis, the work could never have passed muster except as a whole; nor did his critics match the breadth of his compilation of ethnobotanical material from the ancient Classical sources. [...]

Wasson had in his hands a paper by the brilliant Russian linguist, Vladimir Nikolaevic Topovov [sic—Toporov], that should have laid the basis for a reexamination of Allegro's etymologies. [Ruck then goes into a page of etymological descriptions of Toporov's work showing its support for Allegro.]
~ Carl Ruck, *Fungus Redivivus*

Wasson continues: "When he occasionally touches on subjects with which I am familiar, as the Plaincourault fresco and the chemistry of the fly-agaric, he is, well, unimpressive."

If we unquestioningly agree with Wasson's contradictory and shaky, if not downright dishonest, position regarding the Plaincourault fresco, then his argument, at least on the surface, appears logical. But as has already been shown (Hoffman et al, 2006; Ruck et al, 2007/2005/2001; Samorini, 1998), the Wasson-Panofsky argument against the Plaincourault fresco as *Amanita* is unfounded.

Wasson closes his letter with an insult to Allegro, calling him: an "Anglo-Saxon mycophobe" because "The peoples of the Near and Middle East about whom Mr. Allegro is writing were among the most gifted and sophisticated that mankind has produced". As mentioned before, and as I'll further show, Allegro based his descriptions of the mushroom's effects mostly on those of people that Wasson himself had worked with. And Wasson is saying this of Allegro—a man who spent years in the Middle East translating the Dead Sea Scrolls.

This leaves Wasson with one valid contention remaining against Allegro, the issue of the chemistry of the fly-agaric. To examine the schism further, we will review exactly what Allegro's sources were.

Allegro's References and Citations

This section offers critical analysis and commentary on all of Allegro's endnotes and citations in *The Sacred Mushroom and the Cross (SMC)* with regard to entheogens. While careful study of this section will provide the scholar with an in-depth understanding, some readers may wish to skip through and read only the commentaries.

Directly below is a list showing the number of times each entheobotanical scholar is referenced by Allegro in *SMC*. They appear in descending order.

- Professor John Ramsbottom (9×)
- R. Gordon Wasson (5×)
- Robert Graves (3×)
- Dr. S. Henry Wassen (3×)
- Dr. Andrija Puharich (2×)
- Dr. Richard Evans Schultes (2×)
- Waldemar Jochelson (2×)
- Dr. Albert Hofmann (1×)
- Dr. Roger Heim (1×)

The following excerpts are from *SMC* and pertain to entheogenic and entheobotanical studies. They appear in the main text of the book and represent all the specific references to other scholars in the field of entheobotany and entheogens listed in *SMC*. Also provided is each endnote connected with the main text and, with a few exceptions, each citation connected with the endnote. The excluded citations are as follows:

- One citation to Wasson—*Soma*—discussed but excluded for brevity.
- One citation to John Ramsbottom—discussed but excluded for brevity.
- Three citations to Henry Wassen—discussed but excluded for brevity.
- One citation to Heim and Wasson on Psilocybin—not important to our study.

- One citation to Albert Hofmann on Psilocybin – not important to our study.

Citations to Professor John Ramsbottom
(*Mushrooms & Toadstools*, 1953/1954):

> Ch. V, Pg. 231, endnote #19
> Ch. VII, Pg. 241, endnote #2, #5
> Ch. VII, Pg. 242, endnote #10
> Ch. IX, Pg. 253, endnote #20
> Ch. X, Pg. 256, endnote #27
> Ch. XIV, Pg. 277, endnote #32
> Ch. XVII, Pg. 299, endnote #94
> Ch. XVIII, Pg. 301, endnote #5

From *The Sacred Mushroom and the Cross*
Ch. V, pg. 40:
Even among the Greek and Roman botanical works there are scarcely a dozen different words which have been recognized as relating specifically to the fungus, and the whole of extant Semitic literature can produce few more. Mycology, as the study of fungi is called after the Greek mukes, "mushroom", is a comparatively modern science. **(19)**

Ch. V, Pg. 231, endnote #19:
For a useful summary, see J. Ramsbottom, *Mushrooms & Toadstools*, London, 1953, ch.3

Ramsbottom: ch. 3 [Omitted]
Chapter 3 in Ramsbottom's book *Mushrooms & Toadstools*, is entitled "History," and is composed of twelve pages of general citations on ancient mushroom history and the development of mushroom knowledge (mycology). See pages 12–24.

From *The Sacred Mushroom and the Cross*
Ch. VII, pg. 54:

More prosaically, perhaps, the process is thus described by a modern mycologist: "In the genus Amanita a membrane surrounds the young fungus. In addition to this wrapper or volva there is another membrane, stretching from the margin of the cap and joined to the stem, as in the mushroom. Thus it is as if the "button stage" were surrounded by an outer skin. As the fungus develops this is torn apart. If its texture is sufficiently tenacious to hold it together, it is left as a cup at the base of the stem . . . With growth the membrane covering the gills tears and is left as a ring on the stem." Of the Amanita phalloides, the writer adds:

"Before the volva breaks the fungus looks somewhat like a pigeon's egg half-buried, or like a small phallus 'egg'. It is common in glades in woods and adjoining pastures after the first summer rains, and continues through early autumn. **(2)**

Ch. VII, Pg. 241, endnote #2:
J. Ramsbottom op. cit. p. 39.

Ramsbottom pg. 39:

In the genus Amanita a membrane surrounds the young fungus. In addition to this wrapper or vulva three is another membrane, stretching from the margin of the cap and joined to the stem, as in the mushroom. Thus it is as if the "button stage" were surrounded by an outer skin. As the fungus develops this is torn apart. If its texture is sufficiently tenacious to hold together, it is left as a cup at the base of the stem (A. phalloides); if it is friable the part covering the cap remains there and becomes broken up into wart-like particles (A. muscaria, A. pantherina). An intermediate type is seen in A. mappa. With growth the membrane covering the gills tears and is left as a ring on the stem. The spores are white and the gills in most species are also white: they do not quite reach the stem.

Amanita phalloides has a hemispherical, then flattened, greenish olive silky cap with blackish fibrils radiating from the centre;

occasionally it is more yellowish or brownish or even whitish. The gills, stem and ring are white, but may have a slight greenish tinge. It has no particular smell or taste. Before the volva breaks the fungus looks somewhat like a pigeon's egg half-buried, or like a small phallus "egg".

From *The Sacred Mushroom and the Cross*
Ch. VII, pg. 54–55:
Until the invention of the microscope the function of the spore, produced by each fungus in its millions, could not be appreciated. The mushroom has, indeed, no seed in the accepted sense, germinating and giving out a root and later a stem apex with or without seed leaves. The walls of each minute spore extrude to form thread-like tubes which branch further until all mass together to form the spongy flesh of the fungus. The result is neither animal nor vegetable, and the mystery of its proper classification persisted until relatively modern times. Thus a sixteenth-century naturalist wrote: "They are a sort of intermediate existence between plants and inanimate nature. In this respect fungi resemble zoophytes, which are intermediate between plants and animals." **(5)**

Ch. VII, Pg. 241, endnote #5:
Caesalpinus in De Plantis, 1583; qu. Ramsbottom op. cit. p. 14.

Ramsbottom pg. 14:
The earlier herbalists were occupied for the main part in elucidating De Materia Medica of Dioscorides. Their interpretations were not simply literary exercises but commentaries with reference to the floras of their own countries, which became more and more valuable as it was gradually realised that many of the plants were different, and illustrations were made from living specimens. William Turner in A new Herball (1551–1568), the first important English botanical work, realised the difficulties, and in his forthright manner—wrote that he had:

"taught the truthe of certyne plantes... And because I would not be lyke unto a cryer yt cryeth a loste horse in the marketh, & telleth all the markes and tokens that he hath, & yet never sawe the horse, nether coulde knowe the horse if he sawe him: I wente into Italye and into diverse partes of Germany, to knowe and se the herbes my selfe."

Mixed with ideas about the nature of fungi which are derived directly from writers of antiquity, we find modifications due to personal observations and independent judgment. Thus Caesalpinus in De Plantis (1583), wrote that:

"Some plants have no seed; these are the most imperfect, and spring from decaying substances; and they therefore have to feed themselves and grow, and are unable to produce their like; they are a sort of intermediate existence between plants and inanimate nature. In this respect fungi resemble zoophytes, which are intermediate between plants and animals."

Here we have a fairly clear statement that fungi arise spontaneously and a suggestion that they are not plants. They played a notable part in the controversies about spontaneous generation, which held on, with shifting ground of argument, until almost the end of the last century. Whether fungi are plants or not depends upon definition. The question repeatedly arose, and several, like Linnaeus, thought fungi might form a new natural kingdom between those of plants and animals.

From *The Sacred Mushroom and the Cross*
Ch. VII, pg. 56:
The slimy juice of the mushroom which, in some phalloidic species, spills over the "glans" and down the stem, seemed to the ancients like the viscous exudation of the genital organs prior to coitus and the seminal discharge at orgasm. The Hebrew word for "smooth, slimy" derives from a Sumerian phrase meaning "semen running to waste", and figures in a number of biblical allusions to the mushroom. It was otherwise known as "spittle", and Job asks if there is any taste in the

"spittle of the mushroom" (as we should now read the name of that plant) (Job 6:6). **(10)**

Ch. VII, pg. 242, endnote #10:

[...] ("viscous gummy moisture from trees from which fungi are derived", and the tradition among the Koryaks (↑V n. 12) that the mushroom was derived from the god who spat on the earth, and out of his saliva agaric appeared. Note also the Polish story that mushrooms appeared where the apostle Peter spat on the ground as he walked behind Jesus (qu. Ramsbottom op. cit. pg. 45)); [...]

Ramsbottom pg. 45:

There is a tradition that the Vikings sought its aid to go berserk— apparently started by S. Ödman in 1784—and stories were told in the days of prohibition in U.S.A., that it was found less expensive and just as effective as boot-leg liquor. What would doubtless be regarded as a fable but for its repeated confirmation over two centuries, is the use made of the fungus by the Koryak and neighbouring tribes of Kamchatka: [...] * [...] all refer to it. W.I. Jochelsen [sic], in 1900-01, carried out a study of the Koryak tribes. The Fly-Agaric is among the objects believed by the Koryak to be endowed with particular power.

"Once, so the Koryak relate, Big-Raven had caught a whale, and could not send it to its home in the sea. He was unable to lift the grass bag containing traveling-provisions for the whale. Big-Raven applied to Existence (Yahiynin) to help him. The deity said to him, 'Go to a level place near the sea: there thou wilt find white soft stalks with spotted hats. These are the spirits wapaq. Eat some of them, and they will help thee. Big-Raven went. Then the Supreme Being spat upon the earth, and out of his saliva the agaric appeared.† Big-Raven found the fungus, ate of it, and began to feel gay. He started to dance. The Fly-Agaric said to him, 'How is it that thou, being such a strong man, canst not lift the bag?'—'That is right' said Big-Raven. 'I am a strong man. I shall go and lift the traveling-bag.' He went, lifted the bag at once, and sent the whale home. Then the Agaric showed him how the whale was going out to sea, and how he would return to his comrades. Then Big-Raven said 'Let the Agaric remain on earth, and let my children see what it will show them.' "

The Koryak's idea is that a person drugged with the fungus does what the spirits residing in it tell him to do.

* It is apparently from Strahlenberg that Oliver Goldsmith derives the account given in Letters from a Citizen of the World to his friends in the East.

† This recalls the tradition current in Poland and adjoining regions. When Christ and Peter were passing through a forest after a long journey without food, Peter, who had a loaf in his sack but did not take it out for fear of offending his Master, slipped a piece in his mouth. Christ, who was in front, spoke to him at that moment and Peter spat out so that he could answer. This occurred several times until the loaf was finished. Wherever Peter spat out, edible fungi appeared. The devil who was walking behind saw this and decided to go one better by producing brighter and more highly coloured mushrooms. He spat mouthfuls of bread all over the country-side. The wonderfully coloured mushrooms as well as those which looked very much like St. Peter's mushrooms, were however, all poisonous.

Commentary

† This places in question Wasson's contention that the practice was not held since "pre-history," being a modern Polish story. It gives Allegro more cause to question Wasson's conclusions. Below are three new world accounts on a similar theme, one of them from Wasson.

The Mixe consider the mushrooms extremely wise. This is because they spring from the Earth, which is all-knowing of the past and present affairs of man, and furthermore are said to be "born" from the bones of ancient sages and prophet-kings. Related to the latter notion is the belief that only persons with hollow bones are capable of becoming diviners or obtaining successful results when taking the mushrooms.

Additionally, the Earth mushrooms are considered to be soothsayers, being equated with the blood of Christ. The Mixe believe that when Jesus was on the cross, blood flowed from His heart to the ground. From it issued numerous flowers and many kinds of edible mushrooms. All but the last of these miraculous plants then disappeared. Those that remained are the *Na·shwi·ñ mush.*
~ Frank J. Lipp – *Sacred Mushroom Seeker*, pg. 152

[T]he Mazatecs spoke of the mushrooms as the blood of Christ, because they were believed to grow only where a drop of Christ's blood had touched the earth; according to another tradition, the sacred mushrooms sprouted where a drop of Christ's spittle had moistened the earth and because of this it was Jesucristo himself that spoke and acted through the mushrooms.
~ Peter T. Furst quoting Albert Hofmann

I'm glad to tell you whatever I can about the Mazatec mushroom. [...]
Sometimes they refer to it as 'the blood of Christ' because supposedly it grows only where a drop of Christ's blood has fallen. They say that the land in this region is 'living' because it will produce the mushroom, whereas the hot dry country where the mushroom will not grow is called 'dead'.
~ Miss Pike to Gordon Wasson, *Mushrooms, Russia and History*, Pg. 242

From *The Sacred Mushroom and the Cross*
Ch. IX, pg. 80:
The prime example of the relation between the serpent and the mushroom is, of course, in the Garden of Eden story of the Old

Testament. The cunning reptile prevails upon Eve and her husband to eat of the tree, whose fruit "made them as gods, knowing good and evil" (Gen 3:4). The whole Eden story is mushroom-based mythology, not least in the identity of the "tree" as the sacred fungus, as we shall see. (19) Even as late as the thirteenth-century some recollection of the old tradition was known among Christians, to judge from a fresco painted on the wall of a ruined church in Plaincourault in France (pl. 2). There the Amanita muscaria is gloriously portrayed, entwined with a serpent, whilst Eve stands by holding her belly. **(20)**

Pg. 253, Ch. IX, endnote #20:

Despite rejection of identity of the subject ("rightly or wrongly") as being a mushroom by R. G. Wasson: "for almost a half-century mycologists have been under a misapprehension on this matter" (qu. Ramsbottom op. cit. pg. 48) [actually printed in the second edition, 1954]

Ramsbottom pg. 48:

Not in 1st (1953) edition.

The 2nd (1954) edition states on pg. 48:

Addendum: "Rightly or wrongly, we are going to reject the Plaincourault fresco as representing a mushroom. This fresco gives us a stylized motif in Byzantine and Romanesque art of which hundreds of examples are well known to art historians, and on which the German art historians bestow, for convenience in discussion, the name Pilzbaum. It is an iconograph representing the Palestinian tree that was supposed to bear the fruit that tempted Eve, whose hands are held in the posture of modesty traditional for the occasion. For almost a half century mycologists have been under a misapprehension on this matter. We studied the fresco in situ in 1952." – Wasson, private letter of December 21, 1953

Facing page 34 next to the Plaincourault image it says:
"Fresco from disused church at Plaincourault (Indre, France) dating from 1291, showing Amanita muscaria as the tree of good and evil."

Ramsbottom's additional commentary on the active chemicals of *Amanita muscaria*, **pg. 46-47:**

The Fly-Agaric is one of the easiest fungi to recognise and to describe. Consequently its poisonous properties were early known, though doubtless it had attributed to it powers beyond its possession. In a fresco in a ruined chapel at Plaincourault (Indre, France), dating from 1291, a branched specimen is painted to represent the tree of good and evil (Pl. Ib, pg. 34). Presumably it was the artist's conception of the essence of evil made more terrible by enlargement and proliferation. The serpent is shown winding round the stem, offering the traditional apple to Eve, who, apparently having eaten of the "tree," is shown in an attitude which suggests that she is "suffering from colic rather than from shame." [pain in the abdomen from (in this case) muscaria usage, a well-known side effect.]

The poisons of the Fly-Agaric have been studied for well over a century. In 1869 Schmeideberg and Koppe isolated muscarine, which they thought was the essential constituent. It is present in variable but always very small amounts. There has been much research on its constitution, but it is usually regarded as having an aldehyde base: its formula is probably $C8-H19-NO3$. Its physiological effects are well known—abundant sweating and salivation, augmented intestinal peristalsis, colic, diarrhoea, pupils contracted, myosis, slowing down and finally stopping the heart—but they are not those of Amanita muscaria poisoning. As the experiments were carried out with synthetic muscarine (isomuscarine) it is usual to distinguish that in the fungus as mycetomuscarine. Schmeideberg himself found that the muscarine he isolated would not kill flies, and moreover, realised that it could not be the cause of the observed symptoms. [...] If muscarine is eliminated the fungus still retains its poisonous properties practically unaltered. These are so similar to those caused by deadly nightshade (Belladonna, atropine) that it is assumed to be of the same nature and called mycetoatropine although its chemical structure is not yet ascertained...

Commentary

We've already discussed at length how Allegro used Wasson's comment "rightly or wrongly," above.

Allegro's primary error here was not citing endnote #20 as being from the second (January 1954) edition of Ramsbottom's book, rather than the first (October 1953) edition.

We see Ramsbottom making a similar mistake as Puharich (below), though he clearly states that the "chemical structure is not yet ascertained..." However, here, Allegro cites only page 48, and not page 47, which contains Ramsbottom's light information regarding the chemical analysis of *Amanita muscaria* and more discussion on the Plaincourault fresco. We can properly assume that Allegro had read page 47 because he cites this area of the book heavily, and Ramsbottom's commentary of the Plaincourault fresco starts on the facing page, pg. 46. Regardless, as I'll show, Allegro took the blame for something that we now know was unclear in four of the major publications he cited—Ramsbottom, Puharich, Graves and Schultes.

From *The Sacred Mushroom and the Cross*
Ch. X, pg. 89:

In fact, there was a more clinical reason for the Bacchic lethargy. The poisons contained in the cap of the Amanita muscaria promote periods of intense excitement, accompanied by delirium, hallucinations, and great animation, but these are followed by periods of deep depression. To quote one witness to Amanita muscaria intoxication: "The person intoxicated by Fly-Agaric (a popular name for the Amanita muscaria) sits quietly rocking from side to side, not even taking part in the conversation with his family. Suddenly his eyes dilate, he begins to gesticulate convulsively, converses with persons whom he imagines he sees, sings and dances. Then an interval of rest sets in again." **(27)**

Ch. X, Pg. 256, endnote #27:

Waldemar I. Jochelsen [sic], qu. Ramsbottom op. cit. pp. 45ff.; cp. Jochelsen [sic], *Jesup N. Pacific Expedition Series vol. IX: The Yukaghir and Yukaghirized Fungus* [sic] (American Museum of Natural History), N.Y., 1926

Ramsbottom pg. 45-6:

The Koryak are most passionate consumers of the poisonous crimson fly-agaric, even more so than the related Kamchadal and Chukchee, probably because the fungus is most common in their territory," and a very profitable trade results from gathering and drying it. "The Koryak do not eat the fly-agaric fresh. The poison is then more effective, and kills more speedily. The Koryak say that three fresh fungi suffice to kill a person. Accordingly, fly-agaric is dried in the sun or over the hearth after it has been gathered. It is eaten by men only; at least, I never saw a woman drugged by it. The method of using it varies*. As far as I could see [...] the men, before eating it, first let the women chew it, and then swallow it [...] the alkaloid of fly-agaric produces intoxication, hallucinations, and delirium. Light forms of intoxication are accompanied by a certain degree of animation and some spontaneity of movements. Many shamans, previous to their séances, eat fly-agaric in order to get into ecstatic states. [...] Under strong intoxication, the senses become deranged; surrounding objects appear either very large or very small, hallucinations set in, spontaneous movements, and convulsions. So far as I could observe, attacks of great animation alternate with moments of deep depression. The person intoxicated by fly-agaric sits quietly rocking from side to side, even taking part in the conversation with his family. Suddenly his eyes dilate, he begins to gesticulate convulsively, converses with persons whom he imagines he sees, sings, and dances. Then an interval of rest sets in again. However, to keep up the intoxication, additional doses of fungi are necessary. Finally a deep slumber results, which is followed by headache, sensations of nausea, and an impulse to repeat the intoxication. [...] There is reason to think that the effect of fly-agaric would be stronger were not its alkaloid quickly taken out of the organism with the urine. The Koryak know this by experience, and the urine of persons intoxicated with fly-agaric is not wasted. The drunkard himself drinks it to prolong his hallucinations, or he offers it to others as a treat. According to the Koryak, the urine of one intoxicated by fly-agaric has an intoxicating effect like the fungus, though not to so great a degree. [...] From three to ten dried fungi can be eaten without deadly effect.

* M. Enderli who accompanied the expedition, describes how a woman sat between her husband and his friend and chewed the fungus, then rolled it between her hands into small "sausages" which the men then thrust to the back of the throat. The Fly-Agaric has a burning and sickly taste, and readily causes vomiting, which would interfere with the men's enjoyment.

Jochelson: "The Yukaghir and the Yukaghirized Tungus," Vol. IX of the *Jesup North Pacific Expedition*. P. 419:

They [the Yukagir.-RGW] do not eat mushrooms regarding them as unclean food growing from dogs' urine. However, according to traditions, they used to intoxicate themselves with the poisonous fly-agaric, which is still eaten by the Koryak and Chukchee. The Yukaghir call mushrooms *can-pai, i.e.,* tree girl.

Commentary

Jochelson's accounts would, for Allegro, arguably provide additional historical references to the *Amanita*'s effects in its natural environment. This could be the reason Allegro chose these accounts over the more modern chemical analysis. Ramsbottom mentions "Vikings sought its [*A. muscaria*] aid to go berserk," and the way in which he quotes Jochelson on the mushroom's effects could be interpreted to support the berserker rage theme. Wasson later attacks this in *Soma,* though the entire issue still appears to be under debate (below). Allegro was criticized for citing a professional mycologist, Ramsbottom, who had not tried the *A. muscaria* himself, and based his descriptions of its effects on Jochelson's report. Why did Wasson blame Allegro for both Ramsbottom's and Jochelson's conclusions? In addition, Ramsbottom misspelled Jochelson as *'Jochelsen'*. Allegro copied Ramsbottom's spelling error and further misspelled Tungus as *'Fungus'*.

The entirety of Jochelson's references to the fly-agaric is included in the exhibits in Wasson's *Soma*, beginning pg. 265. The majority of the material is on the Koryak, cited from: "The Koryak: Memoir of the American Museum of Natural History, New York. A publication of the Jesup North Pacific Expedition. Vol. VI, Part. 1. Religion and Myth, New York, 1905. Part II. Material Culture and Social Organization of the Koryak, 1908. pp. 582-584."

Three sentences regarding the *Amanita* are all we find cited from: "The Yukaghir and the Yukaghirized Tungus. Vol. IX of the Jesup North Pacific Expedition. p. 419." As Wasson states: "We reprint in full what they had to say about the fly-agaric habit [...] – RGW" pg. 265.

From *The Sacred Mushroom and the Cross*
Ch. XIV, pg. 125:
We can now see that it is, in fact, a descriptive title of the sacred mushroom, the Semitic word being a transliteration of the Greek panthēr, our "panther". The reference is to the markings of the animal's coat, described by Pliny as "small spots like eyes on a light ground". The ancient botanists must have used the name of the animal for the fungus, just as today the near-relative of the Amanita muscaria, Amanita pantherina, is so named among modern mycologists. **(32)**

Ch. XIV, Pg. 277, endnote #32:
"Amanita pantherina is very similar (to Am. Muscaria) in its effects and its chemistry. It somewhat resembles the Fly-Agaric, but has a brownish grey or brown cap, darker in the centre, with white spots and striated margin. It grows principally in woods, in summer and autumn" (J. Ramsbottom, op. cit. p. 48. Cp. Pl NHXXII93: "...there is

a dry sort, similar to the genuine (mushroom) which shows as it were white spots on the top, standing out of its outer coat").

Ramsbottom pg. 48:

Amanita pantherina is very similar in its effects and in its chemistry.*

It somewhat resembles the Fly-Agaric, but has a brownish grey or brown cap, darker in the centre, with white spots and a striated margin. It grows principally in woods, in summer and autumn. In some German books this fungus is given as edible owing to confusion with Amanita spissa, which differs in the cap being smoky brown and having smaller, less well-defined warts, sometimes even a powdery covering, and in the stem being slightly striate above the ring and the bulbous base being obconic and rooting.

The real danger, however, is that Amanita pantherina should be mistaken for the much commoner well-known edible species Amanita rubescens, the Blusher, which appears from late summer throughout the autumn. In this species that cap is more reddish brown and the warts are usually less distinct. It is a most variable fungus and both size and appearance seem to be definitely related to the conditions of growth: when growing in dry places it is small, firm and compact, and the warts are well defined; in moist places it is large, lax and soft, and the covering of the cap shows as grey patches, or may even be absent owing to rain washing it off or the cap slipping through the volva. The specific epithet refers to the flesh turning pink when broken. This may take a considerable time in more compact specimens, but in lax ones it can usually be noted as pink spots on the gills, or these may become wholly coloured with age. Further, if the base of the stem is maggot-ridden it will be found to be already pink; many species are liable to be infected with fly maggots, but A. rubescens seems particularly prone to attack.

* It is used in Japan for killing flies and has a popular name, "Hayetoritake," denoting this.

Pliny: XXII 93, Ch.46 (alternative translation by John Bostock):

Some of the poisonous mushrooms are easily known, being of a rank, unwholesome look, light red without and livid within, with the clefts considerably enlarged, and a pale, sickly margin to the head. These characteristics, however, are not presented by others of the poisonous kinds; but being dry to all appearance and strongly resembling the genuine ones, they present white spots upon the head, on the surface of the outer coat. The earth, in fact, first produces the uterus or receptacle for the mushroom, and then the mushroom within, like the yolk in the egg. Nor is this envelope less conducive to the nutrition of the young mushroom [than is the albumen of the egg to that of the chicken.] Bursting forth from the envelope at the moment of its first appearance, as it gradually increases it becomes transformed into a substantial stalk; it is but very rarely, too, that we find two growing from a single foot-stalk. The generative principle of the mushroom is in the slime and the fermenting juices of the damp earth, or of the roots of most of the glandiferous trees. It appears at first in the shape of a sort of viscous foam, and then assumes a more substantial but membranous form, after which, as already stated, the young mushroom appears.

From *The Sacred Mushroom and the Cross*
Ch. XVII, pg. 170:

These "loaves" are simply a further instance of the atoning gifts spoken of by the ancient botanists as "cakes", or "loaves", or "honey-combs" to fill the hole vacated in the ground by the Holy Plant, and more precisely described by Josephus as the Mandrake's "equivalent" necessary for a safe removal of that plant by the Dead Sea. All refer to the mushroom itself by allusion to the characteristic "bun"-shape of the all-important cap containing the drug. When dried and skewered for preservation these fungus "lozenges" were represented by the dehydrated ("massoth") loaves of the "unleavened bread" of the Israelites' Passover food, probably related linguistically if not materially with the mazönes of the Dionysiac "cake" feasts. **(94)**

Ch. XVII, Pg. 299, endnote #94:

[...] Cp. P1 NHXXII98: 'Hog fungi are hung up to dry, skewered on a rush"; Ramsbottom op. cit. pp. 45f.: "Fly Agaric is dried in the sun or over the hearth after it has been gathered". Cp. II Kgs 23:9 for the cultic eating of תֻמצ at high places; here a misunderstanding or interpretation of an original תֻיירטפ 'mushrooms'?

Pliny: XXII 98, Ch. 47 (alternative translation by John Bostock):

All the poisonous fungi are of a livid colour; and the degree of similarity borne by the sap of the tree itself to that of the fig will afford an additional indication whether they are venomous or not. We have already mentioned various remedies for the poison of fungi, and shall have occasion to make mention of others; but in the meantime, it will be as well to observe that they themselves also have some medicinal uses. Glaucias [p. 4431] is of opinion that mushrooms are good for the stomach. **The suilli [swine mushrooms] are dried and strung upon a rush, as we see done with those brought from Bithynia.** They are employed as a remedy for the fluxes known as "rheumatismi," and for excrescences of the fundament, which they diminish and gradually consume. They are used, also, for freckles and spots on women's faces. A wash, too, is made of them, as is done with lead, for maladies of the eyes. Steeped in water, they are applied topically to foul ulcers, eruptions of the head, and bites inflicted by dogs.

Ramsbottom pg. 45-6:

The Koryak say that three fresh fungi suffice to kill a person. Accordingly, fly-agaric is dried in the sun or over the hearth after it has been gathered. [Same as above]

II Kings 23:9:

Nevertheless the priests of the high places came not up to the altar of the LORD in Jerusalem, but they did eat of the unleavened bread among their brethren.

From *The Sacred Mushroom and the Cross*
Ch. XVIII, pg. 178:

The Phalloidic species, like the Stink-horn, Phallus impudicus, rises some three inches in half an hour, and the whole erection is complete in one and a half hours.**(5)**

Ch. XVIII, pg. 301, endnote #5:

Ramsbottom, op. cit. p. 180

Ramsbottom pg. 179-180:

(*Bulliard (1784) says that the egg always bursts with great force and explodes at times with a noise like a pistol shot; and that if enclosed in a glass or earthenware vessel which it completely fills shatters it.)

[...] The emergence of the fruit-body is very rapid, about 3 in. in half an hour; under a bell-jar it is often complete in an hour and a half. That it is expansion, which is remarkable, and not growth, which would be inconceivable, is clear if an unexpanded egg is cut lengthwise: this shows the cap fully formed, but the base of the stem extremely short and compact.

Citations to R. Gordon Wasson

Ch. V, Pg. 229, ft. #15
Ch. V, Pg. 229, ft. #16
Ch. IX, Pg. 253, ft. #20 (cited from Ramsbottom)

From *The Sacred Mushroom and the Cross*
Ch. V, Pg. 39:

As we have said, the first step to discovering the nature of vegetation stories and the particular plant or tree that was originally involved is to decipher the proper names. However, in the case of plants regarded as especially powerful or "magic" like the mushroom, additional problems face the enquirer. The strange shapes and manner of growth of the fungus, along with its poisonous reputation, combined to evoke feelings of awe and dread in the minds of simple folk. Indeed, there must be few people even today who do not sense some half-fearful fascination at the sight of the mushroom, and shrink from taking it into their hands. Since certain of the species contain drugs with marked hallucinatory properties, **(15)**

Allegro reference—Gordon Wasson (1×) et al., Albert Hofmann: Ch. V, Pg. 229, endnote #15:

In southern Mexico recent study of the religious use of hallucinogenic mushrooms has identified at least 20 species, belonging to Conocybe, Panaeolus, Psilocybe, Stropharia, and most important, Psilocybe mexicana; see R. Heim and R. G. Wasson, Les Champignons Hallucinogenes du Mexique (Editions, Museum d'Histoire Naturelle, Paris, 1958); for the drugs involved, see A. Hofmann in Chemical Constitution and Pharmacodynamic Action, ed. A. Burger, New York, 1968, pg. 169.

Commentary

R. Heim and R. G. Wasson, *Les Champignons Hallucinogenes du Mexique*, 1958—omitted. This reference is not important to our discussion because it refers to *Psilocybe*, and not an *Amanita* species.

A. Hofmann in Chemical Constitution and Pharmacodynamic Action, ed. A. Burger, New York, 1968, pg. 169.—omitted. This reference is not important to our discussion because it refers to *Psilocybe*, and not an *Amanita* species.

From *The Sacred Mushroom and the Cross* Ch. V, Pg. 39:

[...] it is not surprising that the mushroom should have become the centre of a mystery cult in the Near East which persisted for thousands of years. There seems good evidence that from there it swept into India in the cult of the Soma some 3,500 years ago; it certainly flourished in Siberia until quite recent times, and is found even today in certain parts of South America. **(16)**

Allegro reference—Gordon Wasson (3×), R. E. Schultes (1×):
Ch. V, Pg. 229, endnote #16:
[...] In Guatemala, 'mushroom stones' may perhaps point to the existence of a sacred fungus cult some 3,500 years ago. In more recent times the use of the mushroom as an inebriant has centred in two main centres: extreme western Siberia, among the Finno-Ugrian peoples, the Ostyak and Vogul; and extreme northeastern Siberia, among the Chukchi, Koryak and Kamchadal. Among the Lapps of Inari in Europe and the Yakagir of northernmost Siberia, Amanita muscaria was used by the medicine-men. It has been suggested that it was the drug that gave the ancient Norsemen that maniacal fury on the battlefield called 'berserker' rage: see V.P. and R. G. Wasson, *Mushrooms, Russia and History*, New York, 1957; R. G. Wasson *Ethnopharmalogic Search for Psychoactive Drugs* ed. D. Efron (USPHS Publication No. 1654) Washington DC (1967), p. 405; *Soma, Divine Mushroom of Immortality*, New York, 1969; R. E. Schultes "*Hallucinogens of Plant Origin*" in Science Vol. 163, No. 3864, 17 Jan. 1969, pp. 245–54.

Mushrooms, Russia and History **by V.P. Wasson & R.G. Wasson**
Pg. 192–3:
Before the 18ᵗʰ century was out, in 1784, von Strahlengberg's compatriot, the scientist Samuel Ödman, advanced the thesis that 'going berserk' in early Norse times had been a state of excitement produced by the fly amanita. The Ödman suggestion was taken up and elaborated more than a century later, in 1886, by the Norwegian botanist Fredrik Christian Schübeler in his *Viridarium Novegicum I*. The Ödman-Schübeler theory took popular hold in parts of Scandinavia and even gained acceptance there among writers of scientific and popular handbooks, school textbooks, and encyclopedias. Indeed, many educated Swedes and Norwegians seem to take the theory as accepted fact.

In 1929, a specialist in the medical history of Norway, Dr. Fredrik Grön, undertook to challenge Ödman and Schübeler. He dismissed the fly-amanita explanation for 'berserk-raging' as weakly founded and improbable, pointing out that nowhere in sagas or other early Nordic sources is there a reference to the fly amanita. In this he has been recently sustained by Professor Magnus Olsen, the outstanding authority today on Norse literature and traditions. Futhermore, the ancient writings of the Mediterranean basin make no allusion to fungal hallucinogens nor is there a single mention of inebriating mushrooms in the voluminous source materials available to us concerning the witchcraft cult. Ödman and Schübeler had relied solely on the analogy of modern practices observed among the Siberian tribes.

But their side of the argument has not lacked champions. On November 1, 1918, the famous Swedish meteorologist H. Hildebrandsson read a paper before the Royal Scientific Society in Upsala in which he recounted an extraordinary episode. It seems that in the war between Sweden and Norway in 1814, some soldiers of the Swedish Värmland regiment were observed by their officer to be seized by a raging madness, foaming at the mouth. On inquiry, it was learned that the soldiers had eaten of the fly amanita, to whip up their courage to a fighting pitch. We have not seen the Hilderbrandsson paper, nor discovered the evidence contemporary with the alleged episode on which he relied, but both he and the society before which he appeared enjoy the highest standing in scientific circles, and his paper was quoted by Professor Carl Th. Mörner, a distinguished Swedish physiologist, whose avocation was the study of botany and the higher fungi, in two of his publications on mushrooms. The Ödman-Schübeler thesis received further endorsement from Professor Rolf Nordhagen, the Norwegian botanist; in an article in the Norwegian newspaper *Aftenposten* of January 11, 1930.

Pg. 274–5:
We have now brought to a close our account of the divinatory mushroom cult in Mexico, insofar as it is known to exist today and is

recorded in the annals. Here we would stop, were it not for evidence of an order different from anything so far mentioned, evidence that, if relevant, vastly extends the former range of the Middle American mushroom cult both in time and space. If this enigmatic evidence really relates to mushrooms, as we believe it does, a cult of the sacred mushroom goes back among the highland Maya of Guatemala at least to B.C. 1000, and in that area persisted for close to 2,000 years, until the archeological evidence fades out in what is known as the late classic period, around A.D. 900.

Commentary

In the above text, Wasson takes a more neutral stance regarding the berserker rage theme. However, later, in *Soma* (below), Wasson takes the position that there is no evidence linking the fly agaric to the berserkers or violence. This will be discussed more in a moment.

"Fly Agaric and Man" in *Ethnopharmacologic Search for Psychoactive Drugs*
By R. Gordon Wasson
Pg. 406:

We possess reliable testimony permitting us to say that in recent centuries there have been two foci where the fly agaric has been used as an inebriant.

1 IN the Ob Valley, in the extreme west of Siberia, and along the Ob's eastern tributaries until they interlock with the tributaries of the upper Yenisei, and along the upper Yenisei. In this region tribes belonging to the Euralic family of languages have been historically dominant, and these are the ones that have been addicted to the fly agaric. Along the Ob and its tributaries dwell the Ostyak and the Vogul, called in the Soviet Union the Khanty and the Mansi, respectively. They are the Ugrians, linguistically the nearest of kin to the Hungarians, who together with the Finnic peoples constitute the Finno-Ugrian linguistic group. The Ostyak and Vogul historically have been great consumers of the fly agaric. Their next of linguistic kin, the Hungarians, have no recollection of the practice,

but *bolond gomba*, a familiar expression or cliché in the Hungarian language, means "mad mushroom," as when one says to a person behaving foolishly, "Have you eaten of the *bolond gomba?*", and this may well be a linguistic fossil dating from a time when the Magyar people still shared in the eating of the fly agaric. Among the Finnic peoples, as distinct from the Ugrian, none take the fly agaric today. However, it is of the highest interest that T.I. Itkonen, a reliable investigator, has reported that according to a tradition of the reindeer Lapps of Inari, their shamans formerly ate it, and that it had to have seven white spots. This places the practice well within Europe's borders, on the assumption that the Inari Lapps have not migrated to the West since they abandoned the practice. In the upper Yenisei the Selkup (a Samoyed people), called in the West the Ostyak-Samoyed, and in addition the southern-most of the Yurak-Samoyed, until recent times still used the fly agaric as an inebriant. [...]

Pg. 413:
The Indo-Aryans and Soma

An Indo-European people who called themselves Aryans conquered the valley of the Indus in the middle of the second millennium B.C. Their priests deified a plant that they called Soma, which has never been identified: scholars have almost despaired of finding it. The hymns that these priests composed have come down to use intact in the RgVeda, and many of them concern themselves with Soma. Lately there have been a number of fresh translations of the RgVeda, better than any of their predecessors.

This plant, Soma, was an hallucinogen. The juice was extracted from it in the course of the liturgy and forthwith drunk by the priests, who regarded it as a divine inebriant. It could not have been alcoholic, for various reasons; for one thing, fermentation is a slow process which the Vedic priests would not hurry.

I have studied these recent translations and it is apparent, I think, that Soma was the fly agaric. There are many touches in the lyric poems that fit the fly agaric as a glove, and I believe there are none that contradict it. To detail them here today would take too long, and I must ask you to wait for my book for the full dress presentation of my thesis.

[...] If I am right, the adoration of the fly agaric was at a high level of sophistication 3,500 years ago (and who can say how much further back?) among the Indo-Europeans, and we are witnessing in our own generation the final disappearance of a practice that has held the peoples of northern Eurasia enthralled for thousands of years.

Commentary

This is the largest citation we find that Allegro made to Wasson. It has provided some of the more interesting details of our discussion, though not only for its contents or Wasson's contributions.

Directly following Wasson's short ten pages in the book *Ethnopharmacologic Search for Psychoactive Drugs,* pg. 405–414, are three articles entitled: 1) Ethnopharmacological Investigation of Some Psychoactive Drugs Used by Siberian and Far-Eastern Minor Nationalties [sic] of U.S.S.R.* by Brekhman and Sam; 2) Isolation, Structure and Syntheses of Central-Active Compounds from Amanita Muscaria (L. ex Fr.) Hooker by Eugster; 3) The Pharmacology of Amanita Muscaria by Waser.

Section 2 of Peter Waser's article, pg. 426, begins:

Centrally Acting Compounds
Atropine and tryptophane derivatives

As we have seen, the oral ingestion of muscarine cannot be responsible for the colourful amanita-intoxication of asian [sic] people described by travelers touring Siberia. Different explanations were given and additional central active ingredients were proposed. The unknown active principle was unfortunately given the name Pilzatropin or muscaridine by Kobert in 1891. The search for an atropine-like alkaloid in amanita muscaria has continued since then. Lewis (1955) reported the isolation of hyoscyamine from amanita muscaria and amanita pantherina in South Africa. Later, Polish chemists made a similar statement concerning their local mushrooms. Regardless of the very small concentration found in the mushrooms (<0.0001%), the symptoms of the intoxication do not fit the central effect of the 10-30 mg of orally ingested atropine or belladonna-alkaloids, as scopolamine. Profuse salivation and perspiration, nausea, vomiting, bradycardy, mydriasis, are found, together with central excitation and delirious intoxication. Even small doses of atropine with hallucinations would immediately block the peripheral actions of muscarine (salivation, perspiration etc.) It would be prejudicial to treat here the pharmacology of atropine and similar bases before the presence of these alkaloids in the mushroom is demonstrated with certainty by chemical methods. Until now this evidence has not been substantiated or repeated by other research groups.

Another dubious proposal as a psychotropic principle in amanita muscaria is *bufotenine* (Table 1). This amine was isolated in considerable quantities from Amanita mappa, and detected in small amounts by paper chromatography in Amanita muscaria and Amanita pantherina (Wieland et al., 1953). When injected intravenously, bufotenine may have some hallucinogenic activity in man. This is denied by other research groups using oral administration of 50 mg bufotenine and intravenous injections of 20 mg. Eugster and Muller (1961) were not able to find bufotenine in Amanita muscaria.

The article continues with a full chemical analysis of *Amanita muscaria.* But Allegro hadn't utilized these three publications regarding the chemical composition of the mushroom. If he had a full copy of *Ethnopharmacologic Search for Psychoactive Drugs,* then it would seem unreasonable for him to have overlooked the latest research into the mushroom's chemical makeup. But by reading these earlier sources, we see that Allegro's position was supported by Ramsbottom (above),

Robert Graves (below), and Puharich (below). Not being a chemist, and seeing how the chemistry of the *Amanita* had been debated for decades, it is possible that Allegro felt the safer stance was to take the older position reinforced by Puharich and supported by the accounts of berserker violence. I recognize that this may appear to be conjecture; however, Allegro's next citation to Wasson further supports my hypothesis.

Soma, Divine Mushroom of Immortality by R. Gordon Wasson
Part Three, Ch. 1: The Fly-agaric in Siberia: the Testimony of Explorers, Travelers, and Anthropologists [Omitted]

Commentary

This chapter reviews the numerous pages of exhibits in the back of *Soma* (Wasson, 1968) that detail Western and Russian accounts of fly-agaric using peoples of Siberia.

Allegro states: "It has been suggested that it was the drug that gave the ancient Norsemen that maniacal fury on the battlefield called 'berserker' rage." He borrowed this idea from Wasson in *Mushrooms, Russia and History* (above), Ramsbottom (above), Graves (below), and Richard Evans Schultes (below). However, Wasson later states: "In these comments of various observers there is nothing that suggests the berserk-raging of the Vikings. Murderous ferocity marked the Viking seizures almost always, whereas murderous ferocity is conspicuously absent from our eye-witness accounts of fly-agaric eating in Siberia. [...] The ardent advocate of the link between the fly-agaric and berserk-raging must content himself as best he can with the testimony of Krasheninnikov [4]: 'The Kamtschadales and the Koreki eat of it when they resolve to murder anybody.' This generalisation is hearsay: had he known about a particular episode, he would have reported it. " (Wasson, 1968, pg. 157).

Wasson is incorrect here. There is evidence to link the *Amanita* with violence. However, it should be recognized that this issue is still hotly debated today (see also Lewis, 2001):

The fly agaric is most certainly *not* the drug of the berserkers. The only psychoactive that is able to produce real aggression, raving madness, and rage is alcohol. The berserker madness was also induced by a beer to which *Ledum palustre* had been added.

~ Christian Rätsch, 1998/2005, pg. 634

Against the view that *A. muscaria* has a pacifying effect, we might cite the report in the *Victoria Times-Colonist*, British Columbia, Canada, dated Saturday 10th of July, 2004, of a young student who mistakenly ingested the mushroom, instead of a *Psilocybe* species, and experienced "a brief, but ferocious rampage through the neighborhood; he sexually assaulted a 77-year old woman, jumped onto a roof and hung naked from the eaves, terrorized another woman by trying to smash through the patio door with a flowerpot, and tore apart the interior of a van he broke into." Police had to use pepper spray to subdue him. The next day in court, he was very embarrassed and didn't remember any of it.

Although much research has been published during the past two decades that disproves Wasson's views about the berserkers, Wasson himself had collected in his files a surprising amount of detailed research (much of it presented here) that might have satisfied other scholars that Ödman's original conclusion was actually tenable.

~ Carl Ruck et al, 2007, pg. 288–90

It is possible that Allegro hadn't read Wasson's *Soma* thoroughly, but only referenced it because of the book's previous mention from Wasson himself in *Fly Agaric and Man* (above). I suggest this only because Allegro does not cite a specific page or chapter in *Soma*, and ignores Wasson's ideas that *Amanita* is not related to berserker violence. Or this could be more evidence to support the idea that Allegro was dismissive of Wasson all along.

It is also important to note that Wasson in *Soma*, pg. 162, states: "We do not know what the drug is in the fly agaric, or perhaps drugs." This is interesting because *Soma* was published in 1968, one year after *Ethnopharmacologic Search for Psychoactive Drugs*, 1967, in which the constituents of *Amanita*, as previously stated, are detailed in the articles directly following Wasson's. In fact, Wasson even references two of these studies (Wasson, 1968, pg. 201).

Without the context of these contradictory statements on *Amanita muscaria* chemistry and berserker violence, including Wasson's own, Allegro's position would seem utterly perplexing. But if Wasson himself is seen contradicting the 1967 research on *Amanita*, then how could Allegro possibly figure out the truth of the matter? Schultes later printed his article in *Science* in January 1969 (below), but he also ignored Wasson's 1968 "corrections" on berserker rage. Wasson's attacks on Allegro in regard to the chemical composition and berserker rage of the *Amanita*, as I'll further detail, are completely unjustified.

Allegro addresses the Wasson-Panofsky interpretation of the mushroom tree:
Ch. IX, Pg. 253, endnote #20: (cited above)

From *The Sacred Mushroom and the Cross*
Ch. IX, pg. 80:
(cited above)
Ch. IX, Pg. 253, endnote #20:
(cited above)

Ramsbottom, *Mushrooms & Toadstools*, 1954 2nd ed., p. 48:
(Letter: Wasson to Ramsbottom, Dec. 21, 1953, cited in Ramsbottom, above)

Commentary

Allegro only cited Wasson's published work four times, and three of those were used together within the same endnote, Ch. V Pg. 229, endnote #16. The fourth, Ch. V Pg. 229, endnote #15, relates to *Psilocybe* mushrooms and is not critical to our discussion. The fifth reference to Wasson, Ch. IX Pg. 253, endnote #20, was quoted from Ramsbottom's book, and judging by Wasson's own words in his September 14 missive to Allegro, was clearly something he never intended to reach the public (above). By breaking down the references and looking at Wasson's influence on Allegro's work, we are able to discern that Allegro was, in fact, more dismissive than anything toward Wasson. Clearly, as Wasson himself admitted, he had minimal influence on Allegro's writing.

Citations to Robert Graves

Ch. III, Pg. 218, endnote #26
Ch. XVII, Pg. 293, endnote #33

From *The Sacred Mushroom and the Cross*: Ch. III, pg. 24:

Perhaps the best known of the old Canaanite fertility gods, Baal, derives his name from a Sumerian verb AL, "bore", which, combined with a preformative element BA, gave words for "drill" and "penis" and gave Latin and us our word "phallus". (**26**)

Ch. III, Pg. 218, endnote #26:

BH [...] <*BA-AL> BAL *heru* 'dig' (cp. AL in ^{gis}AL(-LA) *allu* 'pickaxe, mattock' as a digger, and as a sower in AL-DU 'seed-grain', and in ^{gis}NUMUN-GISAL(^{gis} AL) 'seed-plough':cp. Ugar67:II:10, etc. [...]*uBAL 'mushroom' ?>BH [...] 'mound; haemorrhoid' (for mushroom connections in I Sam 5:5, see R. Graves, 'What Food the Centaurs Ate' in *Steps*, 1958, p. 335, suggesting that the votive haemorrhoids of the Philistines were "golden mushrooms"; cp. Pl *NH* XXII 98 for reputed value of hog fungi for clearing "fleshy growths of the anus") [...]

From What Food the Centaurs Ate, in *Steps*, 1958, by Robert Graves, pg. 355;

or *Food for Centaurs*, 1960, by Robert Graves, pg. 274 [alternative edition]:

And again: that passage in the Book of Kings, about the Philistines sending golden mice and golden emerods as a placatory offer to Jehovah, after being smitten with emerods. My old friend Joshua Podro, a Hebrew scholar, whom I consulted in London, told me that the original word in the Massoretic text, glossed as 'emerods,' is *ofelim*—elsewhere used to mean 'a cloud of noisome flies.' *Emerods* are simply *haemorrhoids*, and there is something amiss with this story. The terracotta, or metal, *ex voto* offerings to gods, made by devotees who had been cured of a physical affliction, never showed the limb or organ in a diseased state—it was always sound; the same tradition continues today in Catholic shrines such as Lourdes, and Monte Allegro, and our Majorcan Lluch. If the Philistines had in fact suffered from haemorrhoids, surely their votive offerings would have shown healthy little pairs of buttocks, rather than the swellings themselves? Yet there is a widespread semantic connexion between mushrooms and malignant swellings on the human body. So, since learned Greeks were pleased to identify Jehovah with Dionysus, and the Feast of Tabernacles with Dionysus's Ambrosia, could this emerod story be a variant of the one told by the grammarian Athenaeus? He records somewhere that the Athenians were once smitten with haemorrhoids for insulting Dionysus. I mean, could the Philistine 'emerods' have represented the caps of mushrooms? Thus: 'we send these golden images of divine swellings, oracular instruments of the lightning-born God, whose power has been revealed in the malignant swellings with which he afflicted us. By our complimentary gift of golden mice we testify to the truly curative power of the God's oracle.' And if the Philistines, originally a Cretan people, still spoke Aeolian Greek, and had not yet gone Phoenician, could the Greek word for 'mouse,' namely MUS (as in Latin), and the Greek word for 'fly,' namely MUOS, have identified the swellings as also beginning with MU-namely KUKETES, or MUKAI? At this point I felt the elastic of my argument stretching a little too tight, and relaxed the pressure. I told myself: 'More hard fact, less speculation, please!'

Pliny XXII 98, Ch. 47
(cited above)

From *The Sacred Mushroom and the Cross*: XVII, pg. 156:

So whatever refreshment cheered the hearts of the Bacchic revellers we may be quite sure that it was not just wine, and the vine imagery of their regalia conveyed to the initiates a more potent means of intoxication than the juice of the grape alone. Very probably it was a dried and powdered form of the Amanita muscaria that they used to lace their drink, and it was with this fiery beverage that they washed down the mushroom tops they chewed. **(33)** In any case, many of the more important Dionysiac festivals took place in winter when vine culture had little to offer as an excuse for a wine-bibbing orgy.

Ch. XVII, Pg. 293, endnote #33:

So already R. Graves, *op. cit.* pp. 319–43; *Greek Myths*⁴ 1965, p. 3.

From What Food the Centaurs Ate, in *Steps*, 1958, by Robert Graves, pg. 319–43;

or *Food for Centaurs*, 1960, by Robert Graves, pg. 257–82 [alternative edition]:

It started on April 13ᵗʰ last year, when our Majorcan postman brought me a regal gift: a signed, limited folio-edition (Copy No. 2) of Valentina and Gordon Wasson's two-volume life-work on mushrooms. [...]

[...] But the fly-amanite [sic] is hot as hot—as I learned at the age of twelve when I experimentally touched a piece with the tip of my tongue; it tasted like liquid fire.

The Korjaks [sic] of Kamchatka regularly excite themselves with fly-amanite, and will pay as much as a reindeer for a single dose. What happens then is that their faces turn puce, and they become possessed of an extraordinary muscular strength, often combined with a lust to kill, and an overpowering sexual desire. The excitement induces not only temporal and spatial delusions—of the sort that fascinated Lewis Carroll's Alice when she nibbled the mushroom—but also, it is claimed, the gift of clairvoyance. Moreover, responsible Scandinavian scholars have ceased to regard the mediaeval Berserk madness as a form of collective insanity; it was deliberately induced, they believe, by the individual eating of fly-amanite. Berserkgang ended suddenly, after Berserks had been outlawed by royal proclamation—in A.D. 1015 (Norway) and A.D. 1123 (Iceland); and the clinical picture is characteristic of fly-amanite excitement as reported elsewhere – though, indeed, the sagas do not tell us how the Berserks felt when seized with ecstasy. Fly-amanite, by the way, does not grow in Iceland; it would have had to be imported from Scandinavia. [...]

If my argument held, Dionysus, who played a part in the Mysteries not only of the Goddesses Demeter and Persephone, but of the Goddess Rhea too, may once have been the mushroom-god. And the fly-amanite may have been the secret agent which sent his Maenads raging, with froth on their lips, across the wild hills, tearing in pieces men and beasts – among them Pentheus of Thebes and Orpheus of Macedonia. Pentheus, according to Euripides, had his head wrenched off by Maenads who included his own loving mother Agave. Orpheus suffered the same unusual fate. Since they died as representative of Dionysus, did it perhaps refer to the necessary removal of the sacred mushroom-cap from its stalk? Dionysus's devotees at first drank beer, laced with the toxic juice of yellow ivy—hence the sacred ivy-wreath-and later took to wine. But they drank this, presumably, to wash down the fiery fragments of mushroom; because to tear even a kid in pieces, such fantastic muscular strength is needed as no beer or wine or mead can provide. [...]

Dionysus's own feasts were called 'the Ambrosia'—repeat, *the Ambrosia*—and took place during the mushroom season. Were they originally mushroom orgies? By eating the divine mushroom, did Ixion, Tantalus, the Centaurs, the Satyrs, and the Maenads become as gods? And, later, did the religious leaders of Greece, meeting perhaps at the Olympic Games which Heracles had founded, impose a ban on excitatory mushrooms (as the Norwegian Eric Jarl seems to have done in A.D. 1015), and make wine the sole permitted intoxicant for the Dionysus cult? An official all Greek ban on mushroom-ambrosia would explain Tantalus's and Ixion's punishment—the sacred mushroom being thereafter reserved for persons of good birth and reputation who could qualify as adepts in the Mysteries. [...]

And since the emblem of Argos was a toad, could 'Phoroneus' perhaps represent PHRYNEUS, 'toad-spirit'? 'Toadstools,' or 'toad's bread,' is a generic term used in England and the Low Countries for all tabooed mushrooms, and a German chemist has lately announced that the fly-amanite contains the very toxin, bufonenin [sic] (from the Latin bufo, 'a toad'), which is secreted by the toad's sweat glands! [...] However, one of the Guatemalan mushroom-stones shown in the Wasson's book, relics of a divine mushroom cult extinct for perhaps three thousand years, represents a toad-god sitting beneath his mushroom. Did Phoroneus teach his fold the use of the fiery fly-amanite? [...]

Another happy thought—the little foxes of *Solomon's Song*! The Shulemite has been amorously addressing Solomon, calling him the turtle-dove in the clefts of her rock, glorifying his beauty and prowess. Then she cries: 'Take us the foxes, the little foxes, that spoil the vines; for our vines have tender grapes!' Grapes have already been used in his erotic imagery—'thy breasts are as a cluster of grapes'—and I think she is saying: 'Now that spring is here, let us go delirious with mutual desire, assisted by a fiery dose of "little foxes," and drink flagons of wine to wash them down!' Although the mushroom season had not yet come, dried and powdered fly-amanite could effectively stimulate these lovers. *

* Something was missing in this argument: why a scarlet mushroom should be called a 'fox.' I have since visited Jerusalem and found that the Palestinian fly-amanite *is* fox-coloured; also that a commando force which helped to win Israel's War of Liberation took the name 'Samson's Foxes.'

From *The Greek Myths*, vol. 1, 1972, by Robert Graves, pg. 9:

Since revising The Greek Myths in 1958, I have had second thoughts about the drunken god Dionysus, about the Centaurs with their contradictory reputation for wisdom and misdemeanour [sic], and about the nature of divine ambrosia and nectar. These subjects are closely related, because the Centaurs worshipped Dionysus, whose wild autumnal feast was called 'the Ambrosia'. I no longer believe that when his Maenads ran raging around the countryside, tearing animals or children in pieces (see 27.f) and boasted afterwards of traveling to India and back (see 27.c), they had intoxicated themselves solely on wine or ivy-ale (see 27.3). The evidence, summarized in my *What Food the Centaurs Ate* (Steps: Cassell & Co., 1958, pp. 319-343), suggests that Satyrs (goat-totem tribesmen), Centaurs (horse-totem tribesmen), and their Maenad womenfolk, used these brews to wash down mouthfuls of a far stronger drug: namely a raw mushroom, *amanita muscaria*, which induces hallucinations, senseless rioting, prophetic sight, erotic energy, and remarkable muscular strength. [...]

On an Etruscan mirror the *amanita muscaria* is engraved at Ixion's feet; he was a Thessalian hero who feasted on ambrosia among the gods (see 63. b). Several myths (see 102, 126, etc.) are consistent with my theory that his descendants, the Centaurs, ate this mushroom; and, according to some historians, it was later employed by the Norse 'berserks' to give them reckless power in battle. I now believe that 'ambrosia' and 'nectar' were intoxicant mushrooms: certainly the *amanita muscaria*; but perhaps others, too, especially a small, slender dung-mushroom named *panaeolus papilionaceus*, which induces harmless and most enjoyable hallucinations. A mushroom not unlike it appears on an Attic vase between the hooves of Nessus the Centaur. [...] At all events, the participants swore to keep silence about what they ate or drank, saw unforgettable visions, and were promised immortality. The 'ambrosia' awarded to winners of the Olympic footrace when victory no longer conferred the sacred kingship on them was clearly a substitute: a mixture of foods the initial letters of which, as I show in *What Food the Centaurs Ate*, spelled out the Greek word 'mushroom'.

Recipes quoted by Classical authors for nectar, and for cecyon [sic - kykeon], the mint-flavoured drink taken by Demeter at Eleusis, likewise spell out 'mushroom'.

I have myself eaten the hallucigenic [sic] mushroom, psilocybe, a divine ambrosia in immemorial use among the Masatec Indians of Oaxaca Province, Mexico; heard the priestess invoke Tlaloc, the Mushroom-god, and seen transcendental visions. Thus I wholeheartedly agree with R. Gordon Wasson, the American discoverer of this ancient rite, that European ideas of heaven and hell may well have derived from similar mysteries. [...]

Commentary

For the first source Allegro cited as *What Food the Centaurs Ate in Steps*, 1958, I instead used the American edition entitled *Food for Centaurs*, published by Doubleday, 1960. The two publications appear identical except for their titles and the page numbers that I have listed above.

Graves offers us his personal account of tasting the *Amanita muscaria* at the age of twelve: "I experimentally touched a piece with the tip of my tongue; it tasted like liquid fire." However, Graves's description is false. Touching something with the tip of the tongue hardly gives a valid description of its taste. I have personally eaten fresh fly-agaric on several occasions, and while there can sometimes be a mild tingle or bite from them, it is usually unnoticeable. They actually taste quite pleasant. I wonder if Graves's own apprehension (mycophobia!) caused his reaction. I also discussed this matter with a friend, who replied: "As one who has a major interest in cooking, my experience is that mushrooms in general are notorious for losing initial fresh flavour and texture very quickly: to the extent they can become thoroughly unpleasant. Furthermore they readily absorb flavour from other things. Carefully exploited this can produce wonderful results in the kitchen. But it can also have horrible effects." It could be that Graves simply tasted, if that's what it can be called, a rotten or contaminated mushroom – that is if we dare trust his adolescent memory in the first place. Children are known to detest all sorts of flavors that are generally not savored until adulthood.

Graves goes on to describe *A. muscaria* causing the "lust to kill". In regard to my own personal experience, this sounds more like *Reefer Madness* propaganda than fact. However, as mentioned, I do recognize that there is evidence that supports the *A. muscaria's* ability to *occasion* violence (Ruck et al, 2007; Lewis, 2001). Regardless, Allegro, yet again, took the blame for the other scholars.

The third citation is to: "*Greek Myths*[4] 1965, p. 3.", and while I could not locate a 1965 edition of this book, in my 1972 edition of *The Greek Myths*, vol. 1, the citation Allegro gives as page 3 is located on page 9, which is the foreword. Graves also mentions this reference in *The White Goddess*, pg. 45, where he states: "In my foreword to a revised edition of *The Greek Myths*, I suggest that a secret Dionysiac mushroom cult was borrowed from the native Pelasgians by the Achaeans of Argos."

Citations to Dr. S. Henry Wassen
(South American 'narcotic snuff')

Ch. XVII, Pg. 296, ft. #68

From *The Sacred Mushroom and the Cross*:
Ch. XVII, pg. 164:
We are unfortunately denied reports of such clinical observations as these in ancient literature. The initiates of the mushroom cult explained such sensations in terms of demonology. They believed that the god whose flesh they were chewing, or whose blood they were drinking in their drugged wine, was actually within their bodies. It was to be expected that his coming and going would be attended with dreadful physical and mental experiences, and the body needed

lengthy preparation for the "trial" by fire. The actual eating of the bitter, burning fungus top, drinking of the laced wine, and perhaps sniffing up of the powdered Agaric-like snuff, **(68)** would be only at the end of days of religious and physical preparation. To obtain some idea of the nature of these preparations and the fearfulness with which they were approached, we may read what Pliny says about the Hellebore. We have earlier noted that many of the mushroom names have come down to us attached to this potent herb, and it is not improbable that what the first-century botanist tells us about the taking of Hellebore similarly reflects traditions which he has picked up concerning the use of the fungus:

The best white Hellebore is that which most quickly causes sneezing.

Ch. XVII, Pg. 296-297, endnote #68:

[...] For present-day practice of narcotic snuff-taking, see particularly the reports of S. Henry Wassen of the Gothenburg Ethnographical Museum, to whom the present writer is indebted for drawing his attention to the practice, and the following works by that author: *The Use of Some Specific Kinds of South American Indian Snuff and Related Paraphernalia (Etnologiska Studier 28)*, Göteborg, 1965, with bibliography; "Om Nagra Indianska Droger och specielt [sic] om snus samt tillbehor" (Sartryck ur Etnografiska Museet, Gotenborg, Arstryck 1963-66), 1967, pp. 97-140; "An Anthropological Survey of the Use of South American Snuffs", in *Ethnopharmalogic Search for Psychoactive Drugs,* Proceedings of a Symposium held in San Fransciso, Cal., Jan. 28-30, 1967, *Workshop Series of Pharmacology, NIMH No. 2*, Public Health Service Publ. No. 1645, US Gov.Pr.Off. Wash. DC, 1967, pp.233-89.

Etnologiska Studier 28—The Use of Some Specific Kinds of South American Indian Snuff and Related Paraphernalia by Henry Wassen—116 pages [Omitted]

"Om Nagra Indianska Droger och speciellt om snus samt tillbehor" (*Sartryck ur Etnografiska Museet,* Gotenborg, Arstryck 1963-66), 1967, pp. 97–140

English: "On Nagra Indian drugs and especially snuff and accessories" (Sartryck from *National Museum of Ethnography*, Gotenborg, Sweden ed. by Henry S. Wassen [Omitted]

Ethnopharmalogic Search for Psychoactive Drugs – **Anthropological Survey of the Use of South American Snuffs by Henry Wassen pg. 233–289** [Omitted]

Commentary

These citations to Henry Wassen total over 200 pages of information regarding mostly tobacco and DMT-based indigenous snuffs of South America. Allegro's reference to snuff and its paraphernalia, while interesting in regards to tobacco and DMT-containing plants, may not be applicable to *Amanita muscaria* mushrooms. However, a single report of *Amanita* snuff used for warfare by the Zulu has been documented (Lewis, 2001). In all likelihood, however, the closest Allegro could come to a psychoactive snuff in the Middle East is the acacia parasite snuff, *Moani*, used by Bedouin doctor-shamans, and a harmala-based snuff reportedly used by some Muslim imams (Sajdi, R., 1997, 2007). The possibility that DMT-based Ayahuasca analogues were used by the Jews and Bedouin of the ancient Palestine desert, including by the Essenes at Qumran, has also been suggested (Shanon, 2008; Sajdi, 1997). Unfortunately, Allegro overlooked the Bedouin, whom he worked with in the Palestine desert for months. Further research into these areas is necessary and may yield fruitful results.

Citations to Dr. Andrija Puharich
(*The Sacred Mushroom*, N.Y., 1959):

> Ch. XVII, Pg. 296, ft. #67
> Ch. XVIII, Pg. 301, ft. #4

From *The Sacred Mushroom and the Cross*
Ch. XVII, pg. 163:

The *Amanita muscaria* is, after all, a poisonous fungus. Whilst not the most dangerous, its drugs have a serous effect on the nervous system, and taken regularly over a long period would in the end kill the addict. Among its drugs so far isolated are Muscarine, Atropine, and Bufotenin. **(67)** The first causes vomiting and diarrhoea, and stimulates the parasympathetic nervous system so that the partaker is capable of great feats of muscular exertion and endurance. The stories which came down of the fantastic strength exhibited by cultic heroes, however mythical the events described, have probably that element of real fact. So, too, the idea that the Maenads in their wild raving through the conifer forests were capable of tearing animals limb from limb, was not entirely devoid of truth.

Atropine first stimulates the nervous system and then paralyses it. It is this poison that is primarily responsible for the hallucinatory effects of the sacred fungus, but also for the muscular convulsions that must have seemed to the bystanders like the demons within, wrestling with the newly imbibed power of the god.

Bufotenin, a secretion otherwise found in the sweat glands of the African toad, lowers the pulse rate and temperature...

Ch. XVII, Pg. 296, endnote #67:

See Andrija Puharich *The Sacred Mushroom*, N.Y., 1959, pp. 113ff.

Puharich pg. 113-114:

A number of problems had to be explored. The first one was the chemical analysis of the mushroom, the question here being the composition of the drugs present within the plant. The second problem was to apply the chemicals from the Amanita muscaria to human beings in order to understand its psychic effects. The third problem was to learn to handle the drug in such a way as to minimize or avoid its poisonous action.

The chemical studies with the mushroom confirmed what had already been found in the literature and did not turn up any new evidence. The mushroom like all plants is a composite of many chemicals. However, there are three chemicals in the Amanita muscaria that are of interest in their relationship to psychic effects: (1) muscarine, (2) atropine, (3) bufotenin.

Muscarine when applied to biological systems shows itself as a chemical whose effects can be divided into a number of phases. The initial effect of muscarine is to stimulate the parasympathetic nerve endings, and this is observed in the vomiting and diarrhea usually following Amanita muscaria ingestion. That part of the sympathetic nervous system which is at the head and tail end of the human body is called the parasympathetic nervous system, and in general it is the one that is stimulated by muscarine.

In has been noted by observers in Siberia that the shaman who uses the Amanita muscaria is capable of great feats of muscular exertion and endurance. It is believed that a part of this prodigious ability for muscular exertion is achieved by the use of the mushroom and that the particular chemical responsible is muscarine. However, after its initial stimulating effect, muscarine then acts as a poison and paralyzes the very nerves which it has stimulated. In this paralysis lies the cause of death from the accidental use of this mushroom.

The atropine present in the Amanita muscaria is commonly known as belladonna and was known to the ancients as the deadly nightshade. Atropine alone first stimulates the central nervous system and then paralyzes it. It causes hallucinations and may lead to convulsions. Curiously enough, atropine is a specific antidote to muscarine; that is, it counteracts the effects of muscarine on nerve-muscle endings which result in the symptoms described above. Therefore, large doses of muscarine can be counteracted by a proper dose of atropine...

From *The Sacred Mushroom and the Cross*
Ch. XVIII, pg. 177-178:
The transient nature of the "gardens of Adonis" is exemplified in the rapid growth and as speedy disappearance of the mushroom. Jonah's "sunshade" fungus was eaten by worms the day after it appeared: "it came into being in a night and perished in a night" (Jonah 3:10). A modern observer of the Amanita muscaria detected its first appearance at 8 a.m. and by 4 p.m. the same day the fungus was fully grown and beginning to rot. **(4)**

Ch. XVIII, pg. 301, endnote #4:
Andrija Puharich, op. cit. p. 111

Puharich pg. 111:
All in all, my early morning adventure was quite a success in that I had found seventeen specimens of Amanita muscaria in two hours. I got to the laboratory at 8:00 A.M. and announced my findings to my colleagues. I told them that all the specimens I had found were newly budded and probably would not mature for at least twenty-four hours. But we decided to check them sooner to see how they were coming along. At three o'clock in the afternoon, which was about eight hours after I had first found these mushrooms popping through the ground, I went back to look at my find. I was utterly amazed; the seventeen mushrooms had become full-grown, and, of these, ten were almost rotten from the heat of the sun and worm infestation. Here I discovered something which none of the books had mentioned about the *Amanita muscaria*. There is a certain small slug of a pale oystery color with two little horns on its head which seems to live only for an Amanita muscaria fest. These little slugs attack the mushroom from the base of the stalk and ascend the stalk in its interior by eating their way along it. This, of course, cuts off vital nutrition from the mushroom, and so it collapses.

Commentary

To further confuse the problem for Allegro, Puharich appears to claim that he reexamined the chemical constituents of the *Amanita* himself:

> A number of problems had to be explored. The first one was the chemical analysis of the mushroom, the question here being the composition of the drugs present within the plant. [...] The chemical studies with the mushroom confirmed what had already been found in the literature and did not turn up any new evidence.

Whether Puharich actually reexamined the chemicals in the *Amanita* or not is of no consequence, though he probably did not. The literature used by Puharich was outdated by the time of Allegro's writing by more than ten years. As stated in *Astrotheology & Shamanism* (Irvin et al, 2006):

> Allegro fell under disrepute among chemists, pharmacologists and psychedelic researchers because he quoted Andrija Puharich (who quoted erroneous pharmacology - Wieland & Motzel, 1953) in regards to the chemicals present in the *Amanita muscaria*. Puharich had not verified the chemical composition himself, and this reflected badly on Allegro.

It would be interesting to discover exactly why Wasson attacked Allegro, and not Puharich, for the chemical composition errors in regard to the *Amanita muscaria*. A focused paper on the subject of ulterior motives within entheogenic scholarship is necessary and might fruit interesting results.

Ramsbottom, Graves, Puharich and Allegro all used earlier sources in wide distribution, though Puharich had stated, or at least implied, that he had done chemical analysis himself.

Puharich was in fact a medical doctor, and should have been capable of chemical analysis, but it appears that he may have intentionally misled the reader by implying that he reexamined the chemicals. On the other hand, as far as I'm able to discern, Wasson said nothing to Ramsbottom or Graves regarding his opinion of berserker rage and violence (above), even though Wasson had contacted Ramsbottom in regards to the Plaincourault fresco to correct this so-called error. It is also not clear if Wasson contacted Schultes, who made a similar blurred statement (below). We can only surmise the possibility that Wasson respected Ramsbottom, Schultes and Graves, but for whatever biased reason, perhaps because he challenged him, had no respect for Allegro.

Interestingly, whether important or not, Puharich remarks on the issue of earning Wasson's respect in his description of their first meeting together, page 66–67:

On February 12, 1955, I did meet Mr. R. Gordon Wasson. Alice had invited him to her house for cocktails. I distinctly remember Mr. Wasson's presence that evening as he walked into the room, a vigorous, not-too-tall gentleman in his fifties, and quite distinguished. He seemed a little hesitant about talking to strangers about the nature of his interest in mushrooms. I could not tell whether he was looking upon us as potential rivals or as newly found partners in this lore which he pursued. But my question was soon dispelled, because as soon as he found out that we were interested in the cultural, or ethnic, side of mushrooms he beamed and brightened and began to speak quite freely.

I soon found that I was dealing with quite an expert. I didn't want to leave any false impression with him, so I hastily informed him that my interest in mushrooms was rather recent and that I myself knew very little about the subject. I told him that I was particularly interested in the possible ritual and religious connotations of the mushroom.

~ Andrija Puharich

Citations to Dr. Richard Evans Schultes

Ch. V, Pg. 229, endnote #16:
Ch. XI, Pg. 258, endnote #14:

From *The Sacred Mushroom and the Cross*:
Ch. V, pg. 39, (as above):
...it is not surprising that the mushroom should have become the centre of a mystery cult in the Near East which persisted for thousands of years. There seems good evidence that from there it swept into India in the cult of the Soma some 3,500 years ago; it certainly flourished in Siberia until quite recent times, and is found even today in certain parts of South America. **(16)**

Ch. V, Pg. 229, endnote #16:
R. E. Schultes "Hallucinogens of Plant Origin" in Science Vol. 163, No. 3864, 17 Jan. 1969, pp. 245–54

Note: This is the same reference as above with Wasson – referencing Schultes' entire article. The most important pages to this discussion are pg. 245–46.

Schultes in *Science* Vol. 163, pg. 245–46:
The hallucinogenic use of the fly agaric (Amanita muscaria) by primitive tribesmen in Siberia came to the attention of Europeans in the 18th century. This fungus – widespread in north-temperate parts of both hemispheres – has long been recognized as toxic; its name refers to the European custom of employing it to poison flies. In recent times, its use as an inebriant has been known in only two centers: extreme

western Siberia, among Finno-Ugrian peoples, the Ostyak and Vogul; and extreme northeastern Siberia, among the Chukchi, Koryak, and Kamehadal. Tradition established the use of fly agaric by witch doctors of the Lapps of Inari in Europe and of the Yakagir of northernmost Siberia. Formerly, the narcotic employment of Amanita muscaria was apparently more widespread, and it has even been suggested that the ancient giant berserkers of Norway induced their occasional fits of savage madness by ingesting this mushroom (7).

In Siberia, several mushrooms, often an expensive article of trade, suffice to cause an intoxication. They may be taken as extracts in cold or warm water or milk, either alone or with the juice of Vaccinium uliginosum or Epilobium angustifolium. Sometimes, a dried mushroom may simply be held, moistened, in the mouth. Among the Koryak, the women chew the mushrooms and roll them into elongated pellets which the men swallow.

From *The Sacred Mushroom and the Cross*:
Ch. XI, pg. 94:
The mushroom imagery is here dramatically evident. The prophet sees the *Amanita muscaria,* its glowing red cap studded with the white flakes of the broken pellicle from the volva. In this skin lies the hallucinatory drug, one of whose properties is to enhance the perceptive faculties, making colours brighter and objects far larger or smaller than their real size. **(14)**

Ch. XI, Pg. 258, endnote #14:
XIV p. 132. "An hour after the ingestion of the mushrooms, twitching and trembling of the limbs is noticeable, with the onset of a period of good humour and light euphoria, characterised by macroscopia, visions of the supernatural and illusions of grandeur", R. E. Schultes 'Hallucigens [sic] of Plant Origin' in Science Vol. 163, No. 3864 **[transposed!]**, (17 Jan. 1969), p. 246

Schultes in *Science* Vol. 163, pg. 246:

"Effects of Amanita muscaria vary appreciably with individuals and at different times. An hour after the ingestion of the mushrooms, twitching and trembling of the limbs is noticeable with the onset of a period of good humor and light euphoria, characterized by macroscopia, visions of the supernatural and illusions of grandeur. Religious overtones-such as an urge to confess sins-frequently occur. Occasionally, the partaker becomes violent, dashing madly about until, exhausted, he drops into a deep sleep.

Since 1869, when muscarine was isolated, most workers have assumed that the toxicity and hallucinogenic properties of Amanita muscaria could be attributed to this alkaloid. Studies have shown, however, that muscarine is a minor constituent which could not be alone responsible. The same is true of the trace amounts of bufotenine reported in the carpophores. Recent pharmacological tests show that the central nervous system activity is due primarily to muscimole, an unsaturated cyclic hydroxamic acid, and two amino acids, ibotenic acid, and the less active muscazone. Since ibotenic acid is a precursor for muscazone, the variation in intoxication potential of the fly agaric may be due to fluctuations in the ratio between these two constituents. There is evidence that still other as yet uncharacterized principles may take part in the toxicity of this species (8)."

Commentary

Schultes repeats the theme, suggesting "the ancient giant berserkers of Norway induced their occasional fits of savage madness by ingesting this mushroom." Wasson challenged this presumption in *Soma* in 1968 (above), though it was ignored by Schultes.

Allegro did not utilize Schultes's research on the constituents of *Amanita muscaria*. Regardless, Schultes is not 100% clear either: "There is evidence that still other as yet uncharacterized principles may take part in the toxicity..." This last sentence likely left Allegro feeling that nobody knew the chemical constituents for certain, so he went with the one person who seemed sure of himself: Puharich. Puharich's interpretation matched with Graves's descriptions (above), as well as the many descriptions of berserker violence.

Also to be seen in the endnote are two errors made by Allegro, one a spelling error, and the other a transposed number.

Other Unsupported Claims

In recent years Ruck and Mark Hoffman have promoted the idea that Wasson was changing his opinion about Allegro and his work, and was frustrated over the fact that Allegro never responded to him:

> Wasson, himself, however, was in the process of changing his opinion. From his letters, we know that he was intrigued with the work of Allegro and frustrated by his unanswered attempt to initiate correspondence.
> ~ Carl Ruck, *Fungus Redivivus*

However, it should be clear why Allegro never responded to Wasson's personal letter. We see that on September 14, 1970, Wasson wrote the personal letter to Allegro, but before Allegro could have received or responded to it, Wasson wrote his letters to the editor of the *TLS*, Crook, and his scathing attack in the *TLS*, both on September 16, 1970. With the September 14th and 16th letters being only two days apart, and before Allegro could have possibly responded, it is clear why Allegro never bothered to respond to Wasson and only further distanced himself from him. Furthermore, why should Allegro bother to respond to someone who clearly hadn't studied his book carefully? Allegro had countered Wasson using his own words. Wasson was furious and only felt the need to publicly attack Allegro. On top of this, Wasson's flip-flopping remark "rightly or wrongly" (as discussed) was enough for Allegro to see the waffling in Wasson's logic.

Both Mark Hoffman and Ruck were asked repeatedly for other supporting evidence or letters from Wasson that show his change of mind toward Allegro, or specific changes regarding mushrooms in Judeo-Christianity and the Plaincourault fresco, etc. Mark Hoffman's most recent responses were wholly contradictory (Hoffman, Aug. 28, 2007):

"...i [sic] know that he [Wasson] was also very eager to return to Christianity. (There is at least one letter where he clearly expresses his desire in this direction.)"

"There is not one single letter [from Wasson] that comes to mind, just a wide and open interest [into Christianity] dating to the 1950's... far too wide to discuss here."
~ Mark Hoffman

Until writing this, I have waited nearly two years for *any* evidence to support their claims. I have not seen anything that could support their claims that Wasson was in the process of changing his opinion with regard to Allegro or mushrooms in Christianity. The only statement I could find that hinted towards any difference in Wasson's public and private beliefs was in *Soma*, pg. 174: "We were still unwilling to sponsor openly the notion of a divine mushroom among our own ancestors." In other words, Wasson admits by saying the word "openly" that his private opinion may be different than what he wrote publicly. However, this statement *may* only be in specific regard to European ancestors, which he states on page 176: "I shall begin by saying where in Europe's past I have not found the cult of the sacred mushroom." He then goes on to discuss witchcraft, the druids and berserkers. I should point out that recently Peter Lamborn Wilson, Christian Rätsch et al, and Ruck et al (2007), have published evidence of mushroom use in each of these practices. And if Wasson's own private beliefs are different than those he holds publicly, why not allow Allegro to further investigate the matter? No other evidence, other than Hoffman and Ruck's mere speculation, seems forthcoming.

I should also point out that Wasson, in letters and his interview with Forte, continued his erroneous and unfounded attacks against Allegro (below). If Wasson had actually changed his mind regarding Allegro and mushrooms beyond Genesis in Judeo-Christianity there would be no reason to continue his attacks.

Additionally, as has been repeated, Wasson in no way corrected Ramsbottom on the subject of the Plaincourault fresco because he himself was incorrect (Hoffman et al, 2006). Other scholars such as Samorini (Eleusis ns 1, 1998, pg. 87–108) and Ruck et al (*Melusina of Plaincourault*, 2005; Conjuring Eden, 2001; *Fungus Redivivus*), have presented evidence showing that Wasson's Plaincourault fresco interpretation was wrong.

As partially quoted above, in *Fungus Redivivus* (unpublished), Ruck postulates that Wasson "was in the process of changing his opinion". He also mentions the schism between Wasson and Allegro:

> Wasson, himself, however, was in the process of changing his opinion. From his letters, we know that he was intrigued with the work of Allegro and frustrated by his unanswered attempt to initiate correspondence. Ruck independently was similarly unsuccessful, except for a polite reply from a man who had withdrawn from the world.
>
> —footnote 45: In a letter to Allegro from his Danbury home dated 14 September, 1970, Wasson wrote: "Though we are utterly opposed to each other on the role played by the fly-agaric, we agree that it was important. I think we can correspond with each other on friendly terms, like opposing counsel after hammering each other all day in court who meet for a drink together in a bar before going home. I wish you would tell me one thing: when did the idea of the fly-agaric first come to you and from where?" (Wasson Collection, Harvard Botanical Library.) Wasson is responding to a letter by Allegro in The Times Literary Supplement (11.9.70) concerning the footnote IX. 20 in The Sacred Mushroom mentioned above, where it is not clear whether Allegro is referring to Wasson or to Ramsbottom, author of Mushrooms and Toadstools, on the subject of the Plaincourault fresco. Wasson had corrected Ramsbottom on

the subject of the fresco, who had added the "rightly or wrongly," etc. to a second edition of his book.
~ Carl Ruck

However, Ruck's statement here is cloudy. He provides no evidence that Wasson was "frustrated." He only refers back to this same September 14 missive to Allegro, while at the same time ignoring Wasson's public attack on Allegro written only two days later to the *TLS* on September 16. In footnote 45 we also see some careless writing where it's difficult to discern if Ruck is implying that Ramsbottom added or 'tacked on' the "'rightly or wrongly,' etc." to Wasson's letter before it was published in the second edition, or if he simply means the addendum to the second edition of his book as a whole. Clarification of Ruck's position would be helpful. We'll assume that he means to add the entire addendum, not the altering of Wasson's letter. Wasson himself already clarified the issue in the same missive:

> "...I had forgotten its text, which I have now looked up [...] and find the words you quote in it."
> ~ Wasson to Allegro, September 14, 1970

As already explained, we can hypothesize from these letters that Wasson knew that Allegro had gotten the better of him by using his own words, "rightly or wrongly," against him. It could be out of resentment that Wasson wrote his attack on September 16, giving Allegro only two days to receive the September 14 letter from the United States and respond—which, of course, was impossible. Allegro, likely shocked over Wasson's reaction, understandably distanced himself from further interaction. However, Ruck incorrectly states that "Wasson distanced himself from the Allegro controversy" (Ruck, *Fungus Redivivus*, pg. 10). In fact, it was Wasson who attempted all contact with Allegro, not the other way around. It was likewise Wasson, as has been, and will further be shown, who stirred much of the controversy over Allegro that Ruck claims he supposedly distanced himself from.

Wasson, never forgetting this potential damage to his reputation, did not forgive Allegro for his private letter to Ramsbottom being brought to light. At the end of Wasson's life, he reiterated his position at least three times. The first was the February 1984 telephone conversation with Herer, previously mentioned, where Wasson stated: "there was not one single word of truth in the book whatsoever" (Irvin et al, 2006, pg. 57; Herer, unpublished, Appendix). The second was in a private letter to Mr. Alan Hamilton, dated July 6, 1985:

[Errors in bold]

Dear Mr. Hamilton:
[...]
you quote persons of various qualities and place them on the same footing. I will cite only two extreme cases. My first instance is Allegro on p. 32.

John Allegro was a brilliant linguist in the Oxford circle, so brilliant in fact that the English linguists elected him as the British member of the international team to examine the Dead Sea Scrolls. He wrote one of the early books on them, altogether commendable, and it sold, I am told, more than a million copies. **Of course it was effective only as a first effort and is not read anymore nowadays. Undoubtedly he was elected to represent Great Britain partly because he came from a Jewish family (of Italian origin).** Later he accepted a teaching post at Manchester University. In the 1960's friends of mine in Sweden wrote me that one Allegro was in touch with them about the role of mushrooms in history. He was following the example of my wife and me, and they wondered about that. Our <u>Mushrooms Russia & History</u> by V.P. Wasson and R.G. Wasson, two large volumes, had appeared in May 1957, and all my friends had known we were working on it. It was accompanied by an article by me in <u>LIFE</u>, and they both had created considerable stir in the U.S,A. [sic] **Allegro's book appeared before my SOMA (1968).** His book, unaccountably, propounded some theses **that all linguists reject on sight: he seemed determined to think that Hebrew and Greek languages were vitally influenced by Sumerian.** He intimated that Egyptian civilization was affected by the sacred mushroom, although no one knew what "mushroom" was called in ancient Egyptian. No one could prove that he was wrong, but there was no <u>evidence</u>, none at all, that he was right. **He mentioned me in his book, but only once or twice,** obscurely, in his notes gathered together at the end. So much for his book. **He committed the impossible breach of scholarship by selling it first to <u>The News of the World</u>,** a scandalous, disreputable newspaper of huge circulation, for which it is said **he was paid either £20,000 or £30,000**, worth then far more than today. **Every week for weeks on end there were 8 column headlines on the front page in <u>The News of the World</u> that Christianity had been proved to be a mask for a phallic religion with Jesus standing for the sacred mushroom. Manchester University dismissed him on the spot and he retired to a disused Manse on the Isle of Man. No one looks at his book (except as a curiousity) any more. I wrote to Allegro after his book came out in an amicable tone,** but he never acknowledged my letter. Poor man! What had happened to him? **He must have had a mental breakdown.**

    ~ R. Gordon Wasson

The third was in his interview with Forte of October 1985 just fourteen months before his death. This interview, which is full of errors, further counters Ruck and Mark Hoffman's contention that Wasson had a shift in opinion with regards to the extent of *Amanita* use in Judeo-Christianity, and his displeasure with Allegro.

A Conversation with R. Gordon Wasson by Robert Forte

[Errors in bold]

Pg. 82-3
RF: Would you comment on John Allegro's work (1970) regarding the origins of Christianity?

Wasson: I think John Allegro was a brilliant man. **He was of Jewish origin, an Italian Jew. Then he went up to live in England.** At Oxford, he was **leader in the linguistic circle, and was** a most promising linguist, and the result was that he was appointed to the panel that investigated the Dead Sea scrolls as England's representative – or as Great Britain's representative. That was a great big honor, and a deserved honor. He wrote one of the first books on the Dead Sea Scrolls (Allegro 1956). It sold more than a million copies but is already outdated by other books. It is solid work and is to be esteemed. Then he took a post at Manchester University.

I heard of him first through friends in Sweden who wrote me asking, "Who is this man, Allegro, writing about mushrooms? He never mentions you, but he is writing about mushrooms, and he is asking us questions about mushrooms." And I didn't know it at that time, but he was someone who was working, Allegro, his name was, and **he hadn't had any publicity at all** [as if Allegro wasn't famous via the Dead Sea Scrolls]. Then along came his book, *The Sacred Mushroom and the Cross*, and **he made the unforgivable blunder of selling the manuscript to The News of the World! The News of the World is the disreputable sheet that comes out only on Sunday in Britain. It is like the National Enquirer is here – a disreputable sheet! He sold it to them for thirty thousand pounds, when pounds were worth more than they are today. He sold it to them and they** came out week after week, with extracts from this manuscript, eight column headlines on the front page, "Jesus Only A Penis!"

Wasson: **His colleagues at Manchester they just... Although they have the security of tenure in England at the universities, this they could not bear. They had to get rid of him.** So he retired to the Isle of Man, a rural island. It is a very lovely island. I would love to spend the rest of my days there. It is just as lovely as this is here. **They speak Manx.** Manx is a Gaelic language, as is Irish, Welsh, and Gaelic in Scotland. **There are only a few hundred people there.** Anyway, I had his address, and wrote him a letter after he had gone out there, and said, **"I should like to correspond with you, if you will correspond."** I never heard from him.

RF: Could you comment on his book?

Wasson: Well, of course, I think he jumped to unwarranted conclusions on scanty evidence. And **when you make such blunders as attributing the Hebrew language, the Greek language, to Sumerian, that is unacceptable to any linguist. The Sumerian language is parent to no language and no one knows where it came from.** It was spoken at the mouth of the Euphrates around the gulf of Persia. It was spoken there, and it became an official language of record, documents were kept in that language, written in cuneiform for a long time. In the Akkadian culture for some centuries it was like writing Latin in England during the middle ages as the official language. But as far as being a parent to Hebrew and Greek, that is incredible.

RF: And didn't he speak about the record of the mushroom in Egypt?

Wasson: I think he did. But no one knows what word was used in Egypt for the mushroom. There are lots of botanical words in ancient Egyptian that have never been identified and perhaps it is in among those words. It probably is among those words, because there are mushrooms in the Nile delta, in season, many mushrooms.

Pg. 85

RF: This is from the first chapter of Persephone's Quest, section sixteen, "The Tree of Knowledge of Good and Evil." You write:

"I once said that there was no mushroom in the Bible. I was wrong. It plays a major hidden role (that is, hidden from us until now) in the best-known episode of the Old Testament, tale of Adam and Eve and the Garden of Eden.

I suppose that few at first, or perhaps none, will agree with me. To propose a novel reading of this celebrated story is a daring thing: it is exhilarating and intimidating. I am confident, ready for the storm. I hold that the tree of the knowledge of good and evil was soma, was the calkuhla was Amanita muscaria, the Nameless Mushroom of the English speaking people. The tree was probably conifer, in Mesopotamia. The serpent, being underground, was the faithful attendant on the fruit. (See my Soma, p 214). Please read the Biblical story [in Genesis] in light of all I have written on the awe and reverence that Amanita muscaria evokes, and how the knowing ones speak of it only when alone together, preferable by night. Gradually it will dawn on you that the 'fruit' can be no other than soma. Everyone mentions the tree but its fruit is nameless. [...]"

Wasson: They became "self-conscious." That is the thing that distinguishes humanity from all other species, "self-consciousness.

Commentary

Allegro was not Jewish, or Italian. He came from English and French stock. His father was born in France to an English mother and French father. Allegro himself was born and raised in England. At one point Allegro even studied for the Methodist Ministry.

No articles by Allegro were ever printed in *The News of the World*. The actual newspaper the series was printed in was *The Sunday Mirror,* which is as reputable as *LIFE* magazine (for a comparison, see 'Seeking the Magic Mushroom' by Wasson in *LIFE,* May 13, 1957). Not a single headline appeared on the front page, nor did any of the headlines state the outrageous claims made by Wasson, "Jesus Only A Penis!" The actual headlines read:

Part 1: BEGINNING THE MOST CHALLENGING BOOK FOR YEARS (April 5, 1970, pg. 9)

Part 2: JOHN ALLEGRO's controversial theory that strikes at the very foundations of Christianity (April 12, 1970, pg. 10)

Part 3: WORSHIP BY ORGY TURNED THESE WOMEN INTO WITCHES (April 19, 1970, pg. 34)

Part 4: ABRACADABRA – the magic phrase hidden in the Lord's Prayer (April 26, 1970, pg. 28)

In regard to Wasson's false claim against the fictitious headline "Jesus Only a Penis!," and his remark to Hamilton: "…that Christianity had been proved to be a mask for a phallic religion with Jesus standing for the sacred mushroom," Wasson himself had dedicated 31 pages to mushrooms and their sexual associations in *Mushrooms, Russia and History* (Wasson, 1957, pgs. 153–184), coming to similar conclusions about other cultures (including Arab) as Allegro did with Judeo-Christianity.

There is no record Allegro was paid £30,000 for serialization rights. No evidence exists to back this claim, though this rumor, apparently started by Wasson, has been repeated many times, mainly by Jonathan Ott. The Allegro estate has searched the archives and found no hint of any such payment. I suggest Wasson was trying to blacken Allegro's name using various untested allegations—why else would he throw in errors about Allegro's background? Unless Wasson, once a powerful banker and vice president to J.P. Morgan, had access to otherwise unknown financial records, he invented his claims, or borrowed them from untrustworthy sources.

> Allegro was paid the princely sum of £30,000 for first serialization rights (Wasson in Forte 1988) and at the time was apparently hard-pressed to pay some debts (Wasson, 1977).
> ~ Jonathan Ott, *Pharmacotheon*, pg. 352

Here we see Ott citing the above interview with Forte, but he goes on to cite "Wasson, 1977" which is listed as "Personal conversations, Danbury, CT." The Allegro estate is not aware of any debts that he was hard pressed to pay. In *Pharmacotheon* (1996, pg. 334) Ott clumps Allegro with Puharich and then characterizes him as a "profit-minded writer [who] was to capitalize on Wasson's ideas":

> ...a more profit-minded writer was to capitalize on Wasson's ideas, as Puharich had done more than a decade earlier. In this case, a philologist named John M. Allegro hastily published a book entitled *The Sacred Mushroom and the Cross*, which purported to demonstrate that Jesus was a mushroom, the fly-agaric, and that the New Testament had been written in an elaborate code designed to conceal the sacred mushroom cult from the Romans (Allegro 1970)! Shades of Puharich! [...] It is probably significant that Allegro, a recognized Biblical scholar, did not present his theory in any scholarly publication, but only in a sensational mass-market book, clearly designed to appeal to

the popular audience and not to scholars. I submit that Allegro, like Puharich, was simply trying to capitalize on Wasson's revolutionary ideas. Like Puharich, Allegro contributed little or nothing of value to the field of ethnomycology...

~ Jonathan Ott

Ott ignores Wasson's own statement (above) that Allegro's "book does not show any influence by us," and does not provide any evidence of exactly how he believes Allegro capitalized on Wasson's ideas, or of his assertion that Allegro "contributed little or nothing". He only makes the assertion, which, unfortunately, was taken as fact by other scholars for more than a decade; and is an opinion that, as of this writing, he still holds to (Ott, 2008). Allegro had to publish in mass-market book form because his thesis was too large and perhaps too controversial for the academic journals he had been accustomed to use for his Dead Sea Scrolls translations. In *The Sacred Mushroom Seeker* (Riedlinger, 1997, pg. 190), Ott repeats the unfounded Wasson-Ott errors, and backs them up with name-calling:

> Perhaps most unfortunate was the appearance of farceurs like Andrija Puharich and the late John Allegro, who spun absurd theories based on the Wassons' research to make a fast buck.
>
> ~ Jonathan Ott

Here is a quote from a curious letter in the Wasson archives at Harvard written by Wasson to a Donald C. Webster at Helix Investments Limited, Toronto, February 25, 1970, discussing Allegro's payment:

> "10,000 for all the British rights, 20,000 the world rights, making 30,000 in all"

This citation provides us a solid history of Wasson discussing Allegro's payment with others even *before* his series of articles went to print in April 1970. How Wasson would have such information and why he would be sending it to investment firms is not within the scope of this study. The £30,000 need be no more than a guess at what a tabloid paper might pay out, and the guess is as luridly sensational as the tabloid headlines he misquotes. Here Ruck also noticed Wasson's hypocrisy and could not avoid commenting on it (*Fungus Redivivus,* Footnote 37*)*:

> Wasson was aghast at the financial profit Allegro stood to gain from the serialized rights by the publication of his book in the *Sunday Mirror* (London), although simultaneously boasting of the success of his *Soma*. (Letter dated 25 February 1970 to Donald Webster of Helix Investments Limited...)
> ~ Carl Ruck

Allegro was never fired from the University of Manchester. In 1970 he resigned of his own accord before *The Sacred Mushroom and the Cross* went to print. He'd had enough of academia and wanted to write freelance (Irvin et al, 2006, pg. 183). His own professor, Professor T. Fish, said he was sorry to see him go (Brown, 2006).

Wasson's statement to Forte: "I had his address, and wrote him a letter after he had gone out there, and said, 'I should like to correspond with you, if you will correspond.' I never heard from him" is misleading. Wasson's actual words, written in the September 14 missive, discussed above, state: "I think we can correspond with each other on friendly terms, like opposing counsel after hammering each other all day in court who meet for a drink together in a bar before going home." As has already been repeated, two days later Wasson wrote his September 16 missive to the *TLS*, publicly attacking Allegro before he could respond.

The spoken language of the Isle of Man is English, not Manx. Allegro moved to the Isle of Man partly to avoid the high taxes on authors in the UK, since he was no longer working for the University.

Allegro never had a mental breakdown. He went on to publish six more books—five of which (*The End of a Road*, 1970; *The Chosen People*, 1971; *Lost Gods*, 1977; *The Dead Sea Scrolls and the Christian Myth*, 1979; and *Physician, Heal Thyself...*, 1985) furthered the research he presented in *SMC*. Allegro's first book *The Dead Sea Scrolls*, went through several editions, including one published just four years before Wasson's letter to Hamilton (see Allegro, 1956/1981).

Wasson published *Soma* in 1968, which was obviously *before* Allegro published *SMC* in May 1970. He is thus confused regarding the publication date of his own book.

Below is a revealing excerpt from *Fungus Redivivus* by Ruck in which he copies Wasson's errors but also reveals several more Wasson inconsistencies:

> Allegro was reportedly paid £30,000 for the first serialized rights of his book in an English tabloid, *The News of the World*, and was accused of unseemly profiteering.[39]

> [39] Robert Forte, "A Conversation with R. Gordon Wasson (1898-1986)": 13-30, in *ReVision: The Journal of Consciousness and Change*, vol. 10 n° 4 (1988). Wasson mentioned this unseemly profit to both Ott and Ruck in personal communication and also accepted the criticism of Allegro's linguistic analysis, although his own languages were only Spanish and English. He was eager to accept the rejection of Allegro on the basis of the fact that Allegro had wrongly identified the toxins in *Amanita muscaria*, although that didn't trouble him about Puharich, and that he accepted the Plaincourault fresco as a mushroom.

Besides the obvious errors regarding the serialization being printed in *The News of the World* (though stated correctly as *Sunday Mirror* in footnote 37, above) and the unsupported statements on Allegro's payment, from Ruck's excerpt and footnote 39 we discover that Wasson rejected Allegro's research because "of Allegro's linguistic analysis, although his own languages were only Spanish and English". Next we see Wasson accuse Allegro of "unseemly profiteering," although Wasson had profited exceedingly well from his *LIFE* magazine publication of Maria Sabina and the Mazatec Indians, for which he destroyed their culture and paid them nothing. I have not attempted to verify what others claim Wasson was paid, but Letcher states that he was paid $6000 in 1957 money. The US Federal Reserve compares that figure to over $44,000 by 2007 standards. Letcher had this to say regarding Wasson's profiteering (Shroom, 2007):

> It is clear that his [Wasson's] motivations became more complex, and more muddied, once he had actually eaten the mushrooms in 1955. Thereafter, his banker's instincts seem to have taken over so that he came home with every intention of profiting from his discoveries. In a shrewd move, he had already acquired the rights to all of Allan Richardson's photos, in exchange for funding the photographer's travel and subsistence costs. But within months of returning he had a meeting with top executives of the Merck Sharp & Dohme pharmaceutical company to discuss rights to the mushrooms' potential active ingredients. [...] it was Albert Hofmann's team at Sandoz in Basle who eventually isolated psilocybin and psilocin, but nevertheless, when Sandoz put its patented brand *Indocybin* on the market, Wasson appears to have been rewarded for his part in its discovery with a directorship of one of its American subsidiaries.
>
> He made several other attempts to profit from his story by offering it to various magazines [...] but after a chance meeting he opted for *Life* instead. Knowing that it would serve as a convenient and timely advertisement for *Mushrooms, Russia and History*, Wasson urged the editors to bring the article out in the May edition of 1957 [...] The editors acceded to his demands

– and advertised the mushroom edition of *Life* extensively on television – with the effect that his book, published a few months later in a limited edition of 512 copies and retailing at $125 [over $917 in 2007], doubled in price [over $1830 in 2007] before all the copies were sold. The article itself netted Wasson the extraordinary sum of $6,000...

~ Andy Letcher

It also appears that Wasson gave out 100 copies of his book to friends and colleagues, which would leave 412 copies for him to sell. In 1957 money that equals $51,500 or the equivalent of a *minimum* of $378,000 today.

Next, Wasson further dismissed Allegro because "Allegro had wrongly identified the toxins in *Amanita muscaria,*" although with so many confusing and differing reports by Wasson and his associates, as was shown above, it's easy to understand how Allegro made these errors. Ruck then mentions yet another Wasson inconsistency: "although that didn't trouble him about Puharich." Wasson further rejected Allegro *because* "he accepted the Plaincourault fresco as a mushroom". Regarding the Plaincourault fresco, Ruck states in *Fungus Redivivus*:

> Although Wasson himself apparently dismissed the fresco, he did so with reluctance and included it as a plate for his readers' consideration in his 1968 *Soma: The Divine Mushroom of Immortality,* in which he advanced the theory that the ancient sacred plant-god of the Sanskrit *RgVeda* was originally this same fascinating and empowering mushroom.

As already shown, there is no *real* evidence post 1953 of even the slightest reluctance on Wasson's part to dismiss the Plaincourault fresco, or Allegro. His attacks on Allegro in the *TLS*, the Hamilton letter, and Forte interview are evidence of that. And as I just quoted from Ruck above, Wasson rejected Allegro *because* "he accepted the Plaincourault fresco as a mushroom," that is, *without* reluctance. The only place that I could find any *real* sign of reluctance from Wasson was in his December 21, 1953, letter to Ramsbottom—"rightly or wrongly". He does not show any clear signs of reluctance after that letter.

Ruck suggests in *Fungus Redivivus* (and I likely agree) that it is from this letter that Allegro noticed Wasson's reluctance to draw the conclusion that the Plaincourault fresco was a mushroom, and from there made his move toward investigating drug use within Judeo-Christianity:

> [Allegro] had drawn the conclusion that Wasson was still reluctant to make, although mentioned in his *Soma*.

I should remind the reader that Allegro went public with the idea that Christianity was based on a drug cult in October 1967 (Anderson, 1967), *before* the publication of Wasson's *Soma* in 1968. Therefore, for the purposes of chronology, *Ruck's mention of Soma is unimportant.* As stated, Wasson's statements in the *TLS* missives (above), written *after* the publication of *Soma*, are enough to completely dismiss any argument for later reluctance. But Ruck references pages 178–180, 214–215, 220–222, so let us take a look in *Soma* to see what Wasson had to say on the matter:

> Pg. 179–180: The mycologist would have done well to consult art historians. Here is an extract from a letter that Erwin Panofsky wrote me in 1952:
> [He quotes Panofsky]
> Professor Panofsky gave the expression to what I have found is the unanimous view of those competent in Romanesque art. For more than half a century the mycologists have refrained from consulting the art world on a matter relating to art. Art historians of course do not read books about mushrooms. Here is a good example of the failure of communications between disciplines.

The misinterpretation both of the Plaincourault fresco and of berserk-raging must be traced to the recent dissemination in Europe of reports of the Siberian use of the fly-agaric. I think the commentators have made an error in timing: the span of the past is longer than they have allowed for, and the events that they seek to confirm took place before recorded history began.

There is no sign of reluctance there, so let's check the next source:

Pg. 214–215: Repeatedly we hear of the Food of Life, the Water of Life, the Lake of Milk that lies, ready to be tapped, near the roots of the Tree of Life. There where the Tree grows is the Navel of the Earth, the Axis of the World, the Cosmic Tree, the Pillar of the World. The imagery is rich in synonyms and doublets. [...]

It is the consensus of all who have written on the matter that the Siberians could not have fathered the myths and practices that they have made their own. Or, to put the thought more accurately, the very idea of such a possibility seems not to have been entertained by them.

On the contrary I now suggest that the source and focus of diffusion of all these myths and tales and figures of speech – all this poetic imagery – were the birch forests of Eurasia. The peoples who emigrated from the forest belt to the southern latitudes took with them vivid memories of the herb and the imagery. The renown of the Herb of Immortality and the Tree of Life spread also by word of mouth far and wide, and in the South where the birch and the fly-agaric were little more than cherished tales generations and a thousand miles removed from the source of inspiration, the concepts were still stirring the imaginations of poets, story-tellers, and sages.

In pages 214–215 we still find no clear hint toward any reluctance. We only find further musings on Wasson's 1000_{BCE} era theory, which continue from pages 179–180.

Pg. 220–222: [...] did the Mithraic beliefs and rites come down from the forest of what we now call Siberia? Let us look again at what is known of the Orphic mysteries, and reconsider the archetype of our own Holy Agape. On what element did the original devotees commune, long before the Christian era? Certainly the overt vocabulary relating to the birch and the fly-agaric carried great prestige over millennia throughout the south and east of Asia: the Tree of Life, the Pillar of the World, the Cosmic Tree, the Axis of the World, the Tree of the Knowledge of Good and Evil – all these were variations stemming back to the birch and the fly-agaric of the northern forests. The Herb (or Plant) of Life, the Herb of Immortality, the fruit of the Tree of Life, the Divine Mushroom of Immortality – these are alternatives ultimately representing the fly-agaric, no matter how far removed the poet or sage or king might be from the real thing. In remote China we have seen the devotees of the Manichaean sect as late as the 12th century eating 'red mushrooms' in such quantity as to arouse the indignation of a pillar of the Chinese Establishment: is not this an echo of Siberian shamanism, not having passed direct from Siberia to China, but tortuously, through successive Middle Eastern religions, until we reach the last of Mani's followers, far from his Iranian home? [...]

In the opening chapters of Genesis we are faced with the conflation, clumsily executed, of two recensions of the fable of the Garden of Eden. The Tree of Life and the Tree of the Knowledge of Good and Evil are both planted in the center of Paradise. They figure as two trees but they stem back to the same archetype. They are two names of one tree. The Fruit of the Tree is the fly-agaric harboured by the birch. The Serpent is the very same creature that we saw in Siberia swelling in the roots of the Tree.

Of arresting interest is the attitude of the redactors of Genesis toward the Fruit of the Tree. Yahweh deliberately leads

Adam and Eve into temptation by placing in front of them, in the very middle of the Garden, the Tree with its Fruit. But Yahweh was not satisfied" he takes special pains to explain to his creatures that theirs will be the gift of knowledge it, against his express wishes, they eat of it. The penalty for eating it (and for thereby commanding wisdom or education) is 'surely death'. He knew the beings he had created, with their questing intelligence. There could be no doubt about the issue.

[...] It is clear that among community leaders the hallucinogens were already arousing passionate feelings: when the story was composed the authentic fly-agaric (or an alternative hallucinogen) must have been present, for the fable would not possess the sharp edge, the virulence, that it does if surrogates and placebos were already come into general use. The presence of the serpent is a happy necessity, for throughout Eurasia the serpent is intimately associated with the fungal nomenclature of the mushroom world, or with particular species of mushrooms, though in nature as it happens they have nothing to do with each other. [...]

If these perceptions are right, then the mycologists were right also, in a transcendental sense of which neither they nor the artist had an inkling, when they saw a serpent offering a mushroom to Eve in the Fresco of Plaincourault. [...]

This is yet another continuance of Wasson's 1000_{BCE} theory, continued from the other pages above. This last excerpt is interesting because Wasson further drives home the point of his theory by asking: "On what element did the original devotees commune, long before the Christian era?" Notice the added caveat "long before the Christian era". It appears that Wasson plugged this in as *an intentional afterthought and diversion from Christianity*. He then goes on: "If these perceptions are right, then the mycologists were right also, in a transcendental sense of which neither they nor the artist had an inkling". Why does he complicate the matter by calling it "transcendental"? He says clearly: "The Fruit of the Tree is the fly-agaric." But he denies that the Plaincourault fresco depicts this same tree. Once again, Wasson places his theory firmly in pre-Christian history, even though the evidence was painted in a late thirteenth-century church. We find no signs of his so-called reluctance. We only see signs of Wasson's typical contradictory and contrived 1000_{BCE} position served up for his own self interest—instead of being honest and admitting he was wrong, which I'll discuss further.

For good measure I decided to check one last source not cited by these other articles: *Ethnobotany: The Evolution of a Discipline, pg. 388.*

> Through the centuries we have heard references to the Tree of Life, the World Tree, the Tree of the Knowledge of Good and Evil, and perhaps other names, always pointing to a tree that is revered as holy, the focus of the religious feeling of the people thereabouts. The tree is never concealed, but it is a pity that seldom has the genus or species of tree been noted. I now make bold to suggest that it is always the mycorrhizal host of *Amanita muscaria.* The "fruit" of that tree is subject to taboo, spoken about only one-to-one, most frequently in the evening by candlelight; it is never mentioned in the marketplace or in mixed company. We must assemble all references to this tree and prepare a map showing where it has been worshipped and by whom. Does the religion of that tree still survive?
>
> ~ Gordon Wasson

This reference was published posthumously in 1995. We can see that even to the very end of his life, holding tight to the Genesis theory, Wasson still refused to admit that he was wrong about Allegro. He never printed a retraction nor suggested the re-examination of Christianity and Allegro's work. He instead appears to act more out of jealousy or resentment toward Allegro for doing what he never had the guts to do – investigate Judeo-Christianity. As if wool had been pulled over his eyes for nearly two decades, he states: "I now make bold to suggest [...] host of *Amanita muscaria*" and then asks: "Does the religion of that tree still survive?"

I propose that *Christianity is the surviving religion of that tree.*

Michael Hoffman and I (Hoffman et al, 2006), showed that Wasson's statement in *Persephone's Quest*, "I was wrong," with regards to mushrooms in the Bible is vague and non-specific. Beyond the Genesis story, no statement exists giving any clear indication as to what extent Wasson further believed mushrooms existed in the Bible.

Ruck said Wasson was in the process of changing his mind. But changing his mind about what? After thirty-three years, between December 21, 1953, and the publication of *Persephone's Quest*, 1986, there is no change of position. Exactly how long should we expect to wait for someone to change their mind?

As previously discussed, if we analyze Wasson's statements to the *TLS* from September 16, 1970 we see that Wasson clearly separated his stance from Allegro's by stating that mushroom usage in Judeo-Christianity was known only up to 1000_{BCE}, a very safe position (however inaccurate the date), which limited the use of mushrooms to the Genesis story of Adam and Eve. But, in fact, he never changed his position, as we see from his words in *Persephone's Quest*:

> "I once said that there was no mushroom in the Bible. I was wrong. It plays a major hidden role (that is, hidden from us until now) in the best-known episode of the Old Testament, tale of Adam and Eve and the Garden of Eden."
> ~ Gordon Wasson

Wasson's circuitous admission "I once said that there was no mushroom in the Bible. I was wrong" serves only to mislead the reader into believing that he actually changed his stance, which he clearly hadn't, at least not during 1953 to 1986. By removing Wasson's two misleading statements in the above paragraph: "I once said that there was no mushroom in the Bible. I was wrong," and "that is, hidden from us until now," his true position regarding *Amanita* being limited to the Genesis story is revealed—completely intact:

> "It plays a major hidden role [...] in the best-known episode of the Old Testament, tale of Adam and Eve and the Garden of Eden."
> ~ Gordon Wasson

We also see from *Persephone's Quest*, quoted by Forte (above), that Wasson also appears to attempt to steal credit from Allegro by stating "hidden from us until now". As will be discussed more in a moment, if Wasson really wrote this in the 1980s then he was oblivious to Allegro's research published in 1970, as well as his own change of position toward Allegro claimed by Ruck and Mark Hoffman.

We cannot assume for any reason that Wasson had intended to use Toporov's paper in support of Allegro, though this is one of the strongest pieces in support of Allegro.

Any allegation that Wasson changed his stance beyond the Genesis story is completely unsupported. The 1000_{BCE} theory is, in fact, the only position Wasson ever held.

> In *Persephone's Quest*, Wasson finally identified the Fruit of the Tree in Eden as Amanita muscaria
> ~Carl Ruck

Wasson had long ago *indirectly* identified the Fruit of the Tree in Eden as *Amanita*, all the while vehemently denying a *direct* representation (above). But Ruck's statement goes against everything Wasson said and did and gives him unjustified and undue credit. This is something that

Allegro and Ramsbottom specifically challenged Wasson on, and were attacked for, and therefore *they* deserve the credit.

The only way Wasson could have changed his mind based on what is written in *Persephone's Quest* would mean that Michael Hoffman's analysis is correct: that Wasson actually wrote this circa 1969, not in the 1980s (Hoffman et al, 2006). However, Wasson's admissions to Herer, Hamilton, and Forte (above) further reveal that Wasson did not, in fact, change his position toward Allegro or Christianity before his death.

> Some months ago I read the Garden of Eden tale once more, after not having thought of it since childhood. I read it as one who now knew the entheogens. Right away it came over me that the Tree of Knowledge was the tree that has been revered by many tribes of Early Man in Eurasia precisely because there grows under it the mushroom, splendid to look upon, that supplies the entheogenic food to which Early Man attributed miraculous powers. He who composed the tale for us in Genesis was clearly steeped in the lore of this entheogen: he refrained from identifying the 'fruit': he was writing for the initiates who would recognize what he was speaking about. I was an initiate. Strangers and also the unworthy would remain in the dark. Adam and Eve had eaten the 'fruit, being led to do so by the serpent, the faithful attendant on the 'fruit', what the mycologists call Amanita muscaria...
> ~ Gordon Wasson (*Persephone's Quest*, pg 76)

There is no maneuvering away from Wasson's 1000_{BCE} Genesis theory. He states "I read the Garden of Eden tale once more, after not having thought of it since childhood". As Michael Hoffman and I pointed out, how could this be true unless written circa 1969? (Hoffman et al, 2006) How could Wasson have spent years attacking other researchers for a book he claims he didn't think about since his childhood? This is an absurd level of sloppiness and inconsistency and is clearly problematic for all of Wasson's arguments against Allegro and the use of mushrooms beyond 1000_{BCE} in Judeo-Christianity. If Wasson's statement was in fact written in the 1980s and not circa 1969, then *it places Wasson's reputation on extremely shaky ground.* It would reveal Wasson as having attacked Allegro for more than fifteen years over a book he'd not read since childhood—while Allegro was a biblical scholar. Remember too that Wasson admitted to Herer that he relied on the opinions of a Rabbi and a Monsignor for his critique of *SMC*, rather than studying it himself (above, and Appendix).

Another article in which Ruck et al, similarly attempts to bestow undue credit on Wasson is in the article *Daturas for the Virgin* (*Entheos* Vol. 1, No. 2):

> Wasson's opinion has been substantiated by considerable further investigation [...] Well known now are the many documented depictions of the Paradise Trees as mushrooms: mushrooms and nothing else. They look like mushrooms and that is quite frankly what they are, not stylized trees, for the mushroom played a role in Christian mysticism and so-called heretical sects.
> ~ Carl Ruck and José González-Celdrán

This statement by Ruck and González is clearly misleading. It gives the impression that Wasson himself wasn't one of the largest barriers to further investigation of entheogens in Judeo-Christianity, forgetting that he attacked anyone for going beyond his indirect hypothesis of Paradise Trees and 1000_{BCE}. Wasson is being given undue credit for the very contentions others held against his stated position while he maintained the safety of his 1000_{BCE} argument. But not only that: Ruck and González have mistakenly conflated the Wasson-Panofsky argument in the same paragraph, as if Wasson's own opinion itself was *not* that of the stylized trees—the Wasson-Panofsky argument! This is in fact the antithesis of Wasson's position. Make no mistake. *This was Allegro's position.*

Unfortunately, Ruck and González also refuse to state emphatically that Christianity has a direct basis in entheogens. Instead, they attempt to recreate Wasson's feeble argument: "the mushroom played a role in Christian mysticism and so-called heretical sects." Now, however, instead of limiting entheogen usage to $1000_{BCE,}$ Ruck and González attempt to limit entheogen usage to "Christian mysticism and so-called heretical sects". As was shown in *Astrotheology & Shamanism* (Irvin et al, 2006), and will further be revealed below, this is completely unfounded, as there is enough compelling evidence to show Christianity itself is based on entheogens. It should also be pointed out that the Chapel at Plaincourault was built by the Knights of Malta, a sanctioned Catholic order headquartered in Vatican City to the present day. They are certainly *not* a "so-called heretical sect".

> ...when it was not possible to collect mushrooms for the Eucharist, the same communion with divinity quite obviously could be accessed through the medium of a surrogate entheogen. The continued reluctance of many scholars either to accept or refute Wasson's conclusion amounts to biased obstructionism; the preferred response is either to reject it, often unread, out of hand, or even better, benign disregard, as a subject beneath contempt, requiring neither examination nor rebuttal, even as the evidence continues to mount up that all of the ancient religions of the Old World, not just the Eleusinian Mystery, had entheogenic Mystery sacraments [...] The original identity of the Tree and its fruit was always restricted knowledge, concealed by metaphors and symbols that only a few could know.
> ~ Carl Ruck and José González-Celdrán

Ruck and González incorrectly give Wasson credit for recognizing mushroom trees in Christian art, when in fact *Wasson is to blame* for asserting that mushroom trees in Christian art are *not* depictions of mushrooms. They further state: "The continued reluctance of many scholars either to accept or refute Wasson's conclusion amounts to biased obstructionism." As I have shown, Wasson's confounded conclusion kept entheogens limited to $1000_{BCE.}$ His own position has been nothing but "biased obstructionism" toward other scholars, like Allegro, who challenged him.

Based on the evidence presented, we can logically conclude that *Wasson is the source of many present-day scholars' obstructive bias* against Allegro and the idea of entheogens in Judaeo-Christianity (see Price and Ott, above; and also Letcher (2007), as examples).

> [Wasson] was desperate to prove his thesis but even so he rejected certain pieces of 'evidence' out of hand. He could find no evidence that European 'witches' had used mushrooms. Likewise he rejected the Plaincourault fresco. So if Wasson, a man hungry for evidence, rejected them then I think we can too.
> ~ Andy Letcher, April 2, 2007

Wasson never admitted anywhere, in all of his published works, that mushroom trees were understood and recognized through the time that Revelation was written.

> I suppose that few at first, or perhaps none, will agree with me. To propose a novel reading of this celebrated story is a daring thing: it is exhilarating and intimidating. I am confident, ready for the storm.
> ~ Gordon Wasson

> There was no storm, and Wasson got off scot-free.
> ~ Carl Ruck

In regards to Wasson's statement: "I am confident, ready for the storm," we remarked in *Astrotheology & Shamanism*: "Fortunately, for Wasson, Allegro had already weathered the storm." (Irvin et al, 2006, pg. 57)

Additional evidence of Mushrooms in Judeo-Christianity

Up to this point I have reviewed each of Wasson's contentions against Allegro's scholarship. Upon critical review, in *every* instance, the evidence has weighed heavily in Allegro's favor, and to Wasson's own detriment.

But now that the subject of the Plaincourault fresco has been properly substantiated as a mushroom (Hoffman et al, 2006; Ruck et al, 2007/2005/2001/unpublished; Samorini, 1998), should we take this iconographic evidence as enough to convince the reader, nay the biblical scholar, of the mushroom's use in Christianity?

Here I submit that in fact we should not—at least not *yet*.

In reviewing all of the entheogenic citations used by Allegro, we still have yet to prove the existence of the sacred mushroom in Christianity. We still cannot state *definitively* that Allegro was correct about the mushroom in Christianity.

In this section I shall provide some of the latest evidence that has surfaced since the publication of Allegro's *SMC* and Wasson's *Soma*. It is the purpose of this section to tip the scales of hypothetical evidence into solid proof, or show either side as unprovable.

First we'll look at the stages of fruit body development for the main types of mushrooms in discussion: *Amanita muscaria* (Table 1) and two species of *Psilocybe*: *Stropharia cubensis* (Table 2) and *Psilocybe semilanceata* (Table 3).

After this I'll provide some of the strongest iconographic evidence available, as well as the date and location (where known) that each piece of evidence was manufactured (plates 1–43). Since the most well-known and hotly debated piece of evidence happens to be the Plaincourault fresco, and since we must now *include* it as evidence, we'll begin the iconography section with it.

Table 1. The developmental stages of the *Amanita muscaria* (fly-agaric) mushroom – from vulva to chalice.

Table 2. *Stropharia cubensis* in various stages of development. The bottom right image shows bluing.

Table 3. *Psilocybe semilanceata*, otherwise known as the Liberty Cap.

Plate 1. The Plaincourault Fresco, circa 1291. Plaincourault chapel at Mérigny, Indre Dist., France.

Adam and Eve are depicted on either side of the mushroom tree. Eve appears to be suffering from colic, a symptom of queasiness after consuming the *Amanita muscaria* mushrooms. The Tree of Knowledge is most often depicted entwined with a serpent. The serpent-entwined staff or tree is a symbol of medicine and drugs, known as the caduceus.

Plate 2. Adam and Eve, etymology of death (*above*). Of fire-bearing stones (*below*). Aberdeen Bestiary, f.93v., 12th century, Scotland.

Plate 3. Adam and Eve, The Fortunate Sin. Exultet Roll, circa 1072, Abbey of Montecassino, Italy.

Here a *Psilocybe* mushroom is shown as the tree of knowledge, with the serpent forming the caduceus symbol of drugs. Two smaller mushrooms are shown in the foreground.

Plate 4. Roasting a salamander. Alchemy, 14th century, Bodleian Library, Oxford, England.

The salamander is as a symbol of the *Amanita muscaria*. Depicted this way, it is the same symbol as the entwined serpent wrapped around the tree, the caduceus. A hybridized mushroom tree is depicted similar to that of the Plaincourault fresco (Plate 1). A man is shown holding a mushroom and holding his head, dancing under the influence of the mushroom.

Plate 5. Story of Creation – Canterbury (Anglo-Catalan) Psalter, 1147 CE, Canterbury, England.

Each segment is a representation from different parts of the creation of the world epic as described in the book of Genesis. In the top left panel, we see the Great Architect as the "Cosmic Christ" with his compass. In the top right panel we see Jesus, creator and lord of magical plants. Some of the other panels depict God (or Jesus) with the book of the law, as the lord over the sacred plants, and as the creator of day and night. One panel depicts a scene in the Garden of Eden with the serpent. Notice that the serpent has entwined the staff (which is actually the stem of a mushroom). It looks a bit like the *Amanita muscaria*, although it does appear to depict an artistic combination of *Psilocybe* and other types of mushrooms as well.

Plate 6. Detail of Panel #3, Canterbury (Anglo-Catalan) Psalter, 1147$_{CE,}$ Canterbury, England.

The red mushroom on the right is the *Amanita muscaria*. The next mushroom is blue, indicating *Psilocybe* mushrooms. Next may be a depiction of a Syrian Rue plant pod, which is similar in color as well as structure. On the left is a depiction of an Opium Poppy shown in the shape of a mushroom.

Plate 7. Detail of panel #9, Canterbury (Anglo-Catalan) Psalter, 1147$_{CE}$, Canterbury, England.

Adam and Eve in the Garden of Eden; notice the serpent wrapped around the tree making it the caduceus, the tree here is actually shown as a mushroom. The serpent, or, the caduceus, the symbol of drugs, is giving Adam and Eve something to eat that will open their eyes and make them as gods, knowing good and evil. Inside the very top of the center "tree" forming the serpent-entwined mushroom-caduceus may be seen little mushrooms.

Plate 8. Adam and Eve. Bible of Charles the Bald, San Paolo Fuori le Mura, 9th century. Rome.

Adam and Eve are both seen lying asleep directly under the mushroom trees in Eden.

Plate 9. Apocalypse-Incarnation. Bernward Gospel, 1015 CE. Dom treasury, Hildesheim, Germany.

The detail of this image reveals a *Psilocybe*-type mushroom tree, with both open and unopened caps. The entwined serpent is present, representing the caduceus—drugs.

Plate 10. Eve given to Adam. St. Michael's Church, Bernward Doors, 1015$_{CE}$. Hildesheim, Germany.

Two mushroom trees are depicted.

Plate 11. Adam and Eve reproached by the Lord. St. Michael's Church, Bernward Doors, 1015$_{CE}$. Hildesheim, Germany.

Adam and Eve are seen covering themselves on either side of a mushroom tree.

Plate 12. Adam and Eve. Ceiling of St. Michael's church, circa 12th century. Hildesheim, Germany.

Adam and Eve are seen eating the fruit of the Tree of Knowledge. The background is the top of a red *Amanita muscaria* mushroom cap, complete with spots. The fruit being eaten by Eve is one of the spots of the mushroom cap.

Plate 13. The Parable of the Sower: stained glass pane from The Poor Man's Bible Window, North Choir Aisle, Canterbury Cathedral, 12th century. England.

Six distinct clusters of mushrooms, and four, larger, individual mushrooms are depicted.

Plate 14. Martin resus-citates a child. Chartres Cathedral, Martin Window, pane 18, 12th century. France.

Martin is pointing upward at the red-topped mush-room tree.

Plate 15. Martin is consecrated as Bishop. Chartres Cathedral, Martin Window, pane 13, 12th century. France.

Martin is pictured glaring at an *Amanita muscaria* complete with spots.

Plate 16. Carmina Burana – Front piece of a German edition. 13th century.

The image depicts five or more distinct mushroom tree designs.

Plate 17. Meditation with blind Bartimaeus (Mark 10, 46–52), Egberti Codex, Fol. 31, 980$_{CE}$. Germany.

The blind man said unto him, Lord, that I might receive my sight (Mark 10:51). Bartimaeus sits under the mushroom tree complete with striations, which provides the vision, or "sight".

Plate 18. The Sermon on the Mount. Gospel Book of Otto III, Reichenau, 1010_{CE}. Folio 34, Verso, CLM. 4453, Staatsbibliothek, Munich, Germany.

The men are depicted worshipping a mushroom-capped tree on the mount.

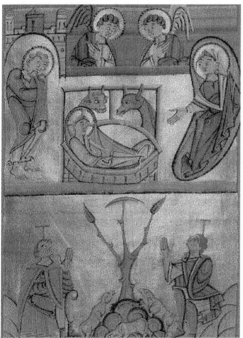

Plate 19. Adoration of shepherds. Thought to be from the Wurzburg manuscript, 9th century. Ireland and Italy.

The center of the tree has a mushroom-shaped top, while the other branches do not. Both men have a red mushroom or 'T' on top of their heads.

Plate 20. Annunciation to the Shepherds, 11th century. Bavaria, Germany.

Two men are seen praying under a mushroom-capped tree.

Plate 21. Profane music. Nave Capital 6. 12ᵗʰ century. Vezelay Cathedral, France.

A spotted mushroom is portrayed under the flute playing the 'profane' music. To the right is some sort of demon, possibly dancing to the music.

Plate 22. St Martin of Tours and the Pagans' sacred tree. Nave Capital 24. 12ᵗʰ century. Vezelay Cathedral, France.

A mushroom is depicted at the top of the pagan's tree.

Plate 23. Death of Absalom. Nave Capital 53. 12ᵗʰ century. Vezelay Cathedral, France.

Two mushrooms are portrayed at the top, inside the tree.

Plate 24. Infant Moses afloat in a basket. Munich Psalter, 1200-1210$_{CE}$, Bayerische Staatsbibliothek, Germany.

Plate 25. Jacob's vision. Munich Psalter, 1200–1210$_{CE}$, Bayerische Staatsbibliothek, Germany.

Jacob lies on the ground beneath three mushroom trees which provide his vision—climbing the ladder to heaven.

Plate 26. Jesus entering Jerusalem. Church of St. Martin, Vic. 12th century. Berry, France.

Plate 27. Jesus entering Jerusalem. Epistolary of Giovanni da Gaibana, fol. 40v. 1259$_{CE}$. Biblioteca Capitolare, Padova, Italy.

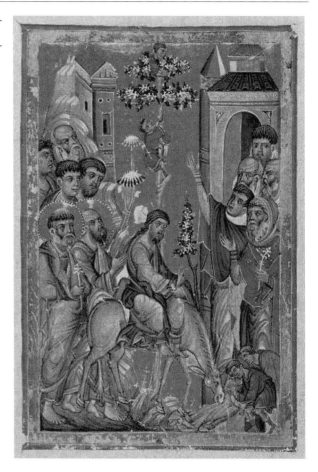

As in plate 26, the mushroom tree is present, complete with striations. However, in this image the focus is not only the large mushroom tree, but what the colt is looking at with gritting teeth—a mushroom.

Plate 28. Jesus entering Jerusalem. Perikopenbuch von St. Erentrud in Salzburg, 1140. Munich, Germany.

As in the previous two plates, the mushroom tree is depicted. Here, as in the previous plate, the colt is seen close to or sniffing the mushroom, or in this case, the mushroom tree.

Plate 29. Crucifixion, Psalm 51, Psalter with Old English Gloss, 1073. Arundel 60, ff.52v–53, England.

Jesus is depicted hanging on the cross, but instead of two thieves, we see two mushroom trees. The tree on the right is complete with spots.

Plate 30. Tree of Jesse. The Winchester Psalter, 1121–1161$_{CE}$. England.

The top of the Tree of Jesse is shown as a mushroom cap. The tree is most often depicted in mediaeval artwork as coming from either Jesse's genital region or his forehead. The tree itself suggests the use of plants for Jesse's vision, and grapes, used in the making of wine, are also depicted. Overall, the common theme of the Tree of Jesse seems to be similar to the Eastern philosophy of the Chakra system, which is most often depicted as the caduceus with the khundalini or 'snake energy' rising—by the use of intoxicating plants.

Plate 31. The Winchester Psalter, 1121–1161$_{CE}$. England.

David and lion, above: David is pictured as a shepherd who rescues a lamb from the lion—underneath an ornate mushroom tree. *Left*: David stands with a crook, with two goats. *Right*: David rescues a lamb from the lion's mouth. Allegro argued the lamb to be a symbol of the mushroom.

David and Samuel (*below*): Samuel is seen holding the horn of anointing (psychoactive mushroom, possibly) oil which he pours over David's head. Jesse stands in the middle, with David's six brothers on the left.

Plate 32. Tapestry image of St. Valburga (Walburga)—Feast Day, February 25th. Date unknown. Abbey of Eichstätt, Germany.

The town of Walpurgis is named for St. Valburga, who was sainted on May 1, 779. Walpurgis may have originated from an ancient Viking fertility celebration. In Finland, May 1 is celebrated as Vappu, a day of feasting and drinking mead (in ancient times psychoactive ingredients were added to mead). May 1 is also connected with fertility and the coming of warmer months, as with maypole dancing. St. Valburga is depicted holding a distinct *Amanita muscaria* in its young, bulbous stage of development, complete with white spots—the key to the "feast" celebrations. The background is red with white floral decorations.

Plate 33. The Last Judgement. Holkham Bible, circa 1320–1330$_{CE}$. England. Add. 47682, f.42v.

The wounded Christ sits flanked by two angels with the "instruments of the Passion". The angel on the left stares at three distinct mushrooms that he holds in his hand; while the angel on the right holds a spear. The blessed on the left with the mushrooms are welcomed, while the damned on the right are spurned and led away by a devil. Jesus is seen with both arms up, a mushroom in his right hand and an unidentified object in his left

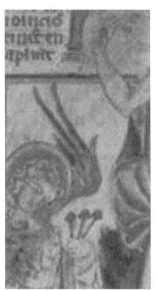

Plate 34. The Watchful Eye, 16th century. Kremlin Museum, Russia.

A mushroom tree hovers over the head of (Jesus?), who is lying inside the vesica piscus, a symbol of rebirth and fertility. The mushroom behind the head, along with the angel, represents the power of vision – the watchful eye.

Plate 35. Trinity of the Old Testament, 1811. Yekaterinburg, Museum of Fine Arts, Russia.

Three chalices are shown on the table filled with a red drink with white spots, symbolic of the *Amanita muscaria*. In the background is pictured a mountain covered with conifer trees, the host of the mushroom.

The detail of plate 35 reveals three red-filled, white-spotted, fly-agaric-looking chalices as seen in the bottom right of Table 1.

Plate 36. Fire Ascension of the Prophet Elijah, 1813. Chelyabinsk Region Picture Gallery, Russia.

By order of the LORD the prophet Elijah withdrew to the creek Cherith and lived there on the bread God's raven brought him (1 Kings 1:1–6). Elijah is depicted on the bottom left, asleep, angel hovering over him, with his head next to a mushroom. Elijah is then shown in various stages of his ascension, or out of body experience, floating up and rising to heaven—depicted as the fiery chariot pulled by four horses. The chariot and horses recalls the myths of Odin and Santa Claus. The Raven's bread has been argued by Edzard Klapp and Carl Ruck to be *Amanita muscaria*.

The detail of Plate 36 reveals a mushroom behind Elijah's head.

Plate 37. Adoration of the Magi, circa. 1569–1649. Juan Bautista Maino, Spain.

Two mushrooms are seen in the foreground in front of the stone. The chalice lies before the mushrooms. Both the stone and the chalice are metaphors for the mushroom. This image was first published by Gordon Wasson (1957).

Plate 38. Genesis and Exodus. Abbey of Saint-Savin sur Gartempe, Poitou-Charentes Region, 11th century, France.

Two mushroom trees are depicted (above left)—the one on the left is severely faded. There is a figure standing between the two mushroom trees, holding up two disks of the sky with figures, possibly the spirit of the lord or Jesus, peering down. A close-up of the mushroom tree on the right shows the spirit of the lord being held above it.

Plate 39. The birth of Eve. Woodcut, 15th century, France. Artist unknown.

Adam lies resting on a mushroom.

Plate 40. Sacrifice of Isaac. Alesandro Allori, 1607. Florence, Italy.

Three *Amanita muscaria* and three possibly *Amanita pantherina* or *Psilocybe*-looking mushrooms are shown in the bottom right. In the field on the left is a man picking plants with an older man watching over him. In front of them are two men asleep on the ground, suggesting they are under the visionary influence of the plants and fungi. The two men walking in the foreground are on the path with the mushrooms. In the upper right is another visionary scene.

Plate 41. Archangel Michael, 13th century, Byzanz (Istanbul).

Six mushrooms are shown under the feet of Michael, and two behind the back of the man having the visions of Michael (bottom right).

Plate 42. Archangel Michael, date unknown. Moldova (Romania).

Michael is depicted in red, white, and blue—the three colors of the mushrooms—complete with the annulus around his waist. Directly above, and to the right of his head are shown the outlines of two mushrooms.

Plate 43. St. Christopher with Christ as child, 13th century. Montferrand du Perigord, France.

On the right of the window is the patron saint of the church—Christopher. On his shoulders is a small figure whose right hand is raised in blessing and who is carrying a cross in his left hand—it is Christ as a child—portrayed as a mushroom. According to legend, St. Christopher helped people ford rivers. One day a child approached him to cross the river. Christopher took him on his shoulders, but during the crossing the child became heavier and heavier, until the Saint had to use all of his strength to fight against the current. The child then told him that he had carried Jesus and that in memory of this he should plant the dry stick that he carried on the bank and that it would bud—a metaphor for the mushroom on his shoulders (or behind the head)—as if to suggest he is under the influence of the mushroom.

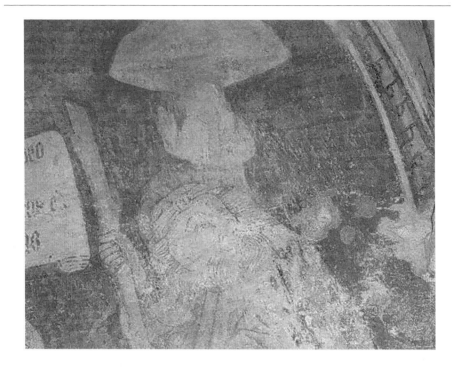

Detail of plate 43 revealing the baby Jesus in mushroom form.

This image was brought to the attention of Prof. Carl Ruck by E. van Roon of the Netherlands.

Consider, for a moment, what it would mean to Allegro's argument, and to further support the above iconography, if we also had written evidence that would give us definitive proof of the mushroom's use in Christianity. Would we not therefore have to give greater weight to the above images as evidence of the mushroom's use? Furthermore, would we not also have to consider the dates of this evidence? And what of its span across Europe from Russia to the British Isles? Would not all of this serve as evidence of widespread use of the mushroom in Christianity? Would not such evidence entirely refute Wasson's caveated 1000_{BCE} theory? Would it not substantiate both the Plaincourault fresco as a mushroom, and Allegro's *SMC*?

I believe that we now have that evidence.

The Epistle to the Renegade Bishops

In an academic journal aptly titled *Harvard Ukrainian Studies* is an article by Professor Harvey Goldblatt of Yale University. In this article (pages 47–75) is found a rare and obscure sixteenth-century Christian text '*The Epistle to the Renegade Bishops*' by Ivan Vysensicyj. This text was discovered in the Ukraine, but was written at the Xiropotamou monastery on the Mt. Athos peninsula, Greece. The text is discussing the forty martyrs of Sebaste, for whom the monastery was dedicated in the thirteenth century:

> (15) There are other miraculous actions which occurred to honor and celebrate the memory of the forty martyrs. These actions took place in the reign of Roman and other pious emperors, who built a holy shrine in memory of the blessed martyrs and adorned it exceedingly. When the names of the forty martyrs were pronounced by the archpriest, there began to grow from the foot of the holy table a holy mushroom with its cap in the shape of forty apples which ascended over the holy table and overshadowed the entire sanctuary. And for this most glorious miracle all present gave glory to God and to the forty martyrs. And then all the infirm found in the cloister were healed through the possibility of tasting the holy mushroom. And this miracle was pronounced throughout the entire ecumene and great multitudes were healed. Thus, each victim of the impious is an abomination before God. The abominable and unlawful Emperor Michael had sought to eliminate Orthodoxy from the holy mountain but had failed, and like Saul had had his house destroyed. Yet Mount Athos flourished as did the house of David. And the monks, who out of fear had hidden, came out and began to sob and weep. And they gathered together the dead and buried them honorably. Thus did the impious emperor with his hirelings perish and disappear forever [87.19–89.14].

The paragraph includes the statement: "And this miracle was pronounced throughout the entire ecumene [...]." Thus, in the only Christian text *so far revealed* in which the holy mushroom is definitively mentioned, is also found admission that this miracle of the holy mushroom of Mt. Athos was announced to all of Christendom.

It should also be pointed out that since the holy mushroom was recognized as such as soon as it began to grow, the pious must have had prior knowledge of the holy mushroom. We do not see them asking "what is this, a holy mushroom?" They state the holy mushroom appeared:

> there began to grow from the foot of the holy table a holy mushroom with its cap in the shape of forty apples which ascended over the holy table and overshadowed the entire sanctuary. [...] And then all the infirm found in the cloister were healed through the possibility of tasting the holy mushroom.

There is no doubt, from the first instance, that it's a holy mushroom.

Therefore, I submit, *against* what Allegro and others scholars have argued, that this was not a "mushroom cult" of the "fringe heretical sects" at all.

I propose that the holy mushroom had a widespread and integrated role not only in Greek Orthodox Christianity but, as the spread of iconography across Europe shows, as a fundamental part of the origins and history of Christianity as a whole.

Judaism and Islam

And what of Judaism and Islam? Professor Benny Shanon in *Biblical Entheogens* (2008) tells us:

Rabbeinu Be'cha'yei ben Asher, a medieval Jewish scholar (1255–1340) famous for his interpretation of the Torah. Rabbeinu Be'cha'yei writes that the purest of foods were created at the very beginning of Creation in order to allow for the attainment of higher knowledge. He explicitly relates this to the biblical tree of knowledge, and comments further that such higher knowledge can also be gained through the use of drugs and medicines available at his time. In addition he notes that the Manna had such qualities as well.

~ Benny Shanon

The latest textual evidence offered by Professor John Rush in *Failed God* (2008) reveals that the Muslim prophet Muhammad believed that manna was indeed the mushroom sent by God to Moses:

We read in Mishkat, book xxi, chapter 1, that Muhammad said, "Mushrooms are a kind of manna which God sent to Moses so that we can see." Some scholars translate this as some sort of eye wash for "sore eyes" (see Hughes 1994:423), but this interpretation is difficult to sustain. The word *manna* (*mann* in Arabic and *man* in Hebrew) in the Qur'an always references some magical substance sent from God (Surah 2:54; 2:82, 7: 160) [...] The word manna, to my knowledge, never referred to some type of simple herbal remedy. Instead manna was used to cure *spiritual* ailments, to convert, through the baptism of fire, the faithless nonbeliever, to make "real," through a hallucinogenic experience, that which can only be accepted on faith.

~ John Rush

This evidence refutes Merkur's argument against Allegro and mushrooms as manna (Merkur, 2000, ch. 1 ft. 5; see also Irvin et al, 2006, pg. 148–9). Thus we may now see a clear history of the use of these substances, *including* the holy mushroom, throughout Judeo-Christian-Islamic religious history.

Up to now I've shown sufficient evidence to prove the mushroom's use in Judeo-Christianity. However, now that we've come this far, is there clinical evidence to prove that the holy mushroom, this "drug", has the physical capability to cause such religious experiences? So many people that I've discussed this issue with wrongfully and automatically assume that the experiences brought on by mushrooms and other entheogens must be similar to alcohol, or that because it's "outside us" they therefore couldn't possibly cause a "*real*" religious experience. But this couldn't be further from the truth, let alone from understanding the effects of the experience. And after all, these substances have been used religiously throughout history by indigenous cultures the world over. Native Americans' use of Peyote is only one example.

In May 2006 a Johns Hopkins University study on psilocybin (the active ingredient in *Psilocybe* species) covered this specific topic. The article by Griffiths, et al, is titled: *'Psilocybin can occasion mystical-type experiences having substantial and sustained personal meaning and spiritual significance'*. It found that:

> ...when administered to volunteers under supportive conditions, psilocybin occasioned experiences similar to spontaneously occurring mystical experiences and which were evaluated by volunteers as having substantial and sustained personal meaning and spiritual significance.

A follow-up study by Griffiths et al, published in the *Journal of Psychopharmacology* in July 2008 confirmed the first study's findings. It found that:

> At the 14-month follow-up, 58% and 67%, respectively, of volunteers rated the psilocybin-occasioned experience as being among the five most personally meaningful and among the five most spiritually significant experiences of their lives; 64% indicated that the experience increased well-being or life

satisfaction; 58% met criteria for having had a 'complete' mystical experience. Correlation and regression analyses indicated a central role of the mystical experience assessed on the session day in the high ratings of personal meaning and spiritual significance at follow-up. Of the measures of personality, affect, quality of life and spirituality assessed across the study, only a scale measuring mystical experience showed a difference from screening. When administered under supportive conditions, psilocybin occasioned experiences similar to spontaneously occurring mystical experiences that, at 14-month follow-up, were considered by volunteers to be among the most personally meaningful and spiritually significant of their lives.

I've included iconographic, textual and psychological evidence, and few grounds, if any, remain for further *cognitive* denial. In the interim I have also shown sufficient evidence to refute Letcher (2007). I shall close with a most appropriate quote from his book (pg. 78):

> The Western rediscovery of Mexican mushrooming practices began, ironically, with a vigorous scholarly denial that they had ever existed.
> ~ Andy Letcher

Conclusion

I have given lengthy discussion to the letters between John M. Allegro and R. Gordon Wasson and discovered that Allegro had indeed technically countered Wasson's first attack to the *TLS* sufficiently, even if minimally.

I argued that Wasson was likely bitter over Allegro catching him in contradiction of himself by quoting "rightly or wrongly," from the second edition of Dr. John Ramsbottom's book. I've shown reasonable evidence to support this claim. Wasson, by his own missives, appears to be more concerned with being on top, or being *the* expert, rather than with discovering the truth in regard to Judeo-Christianity.

The Wasson-Panofsky claim that the Plaincourault fresco has been sufficiently studied by art historians is unsound. To further substantiate this, I've provided additional reference to studies by Giorgio Samorini and Ruck et al, as well as our own study (Hoffman et al, 2006).

There appears to be no evidence to support the idea that Wasson changed his mind with regard to Allegro from September 1970 to October 1985. Professor Carl Ruck and Mark Hoffman's position is mooted by Wasson's own words in his July 1985 letter to Mr. Hamilton and his October 1985 interview with Robert Forte. Further support of my position is provided by Jack Herer, who in February 1984 spoke with Wasson directly. I have likewise shown that there is no evidence to support the allegation that Wasson changed his mind with regards to mushrooms in Christianity or the Plaincourault fresco.

I must say that I do not disagree with all of Wasson's research. Wasson did in fact contribute awesome amounts of valuable research with regards to Rig Vedic Soma use, the 'Mexican cult of the mushroom,' mushroom folklore, the Eleusinian Mysteries and Siberian shamanism. However, Wasson's research into Judeo-Christianity is almost nonexistent. And what does exist is filled with convoluted and contradictory positions and motivations that appear to be based purely in self interest.

Wasson's research should be reviewed on a case-by-case, point-by-point basis, not a blind acceptance. Allegro should likewise be accepted, or dismissed, on a case-by-case, point-by-point basis. He should not be ignored in a blanket dismissal. It should now be clear that each scholar should be given credit where their research is valid and substantiated, case by case, point by point. They should likewise be discredited where their work is convoluted, distorted or laden with hidden agendas.

Allegro did not use Wasson as his primary source, as many wrongly assumed he did. He relied more on Ramsbottom and Robert Graves than he did on Wasson.

I have broken down exactly what errors are attributable to Allegro. As well, I've clarified those errors attributed to the scholars Allegro cited. The errors directly attributable to Allegro are minimal, and largely understandable. The most significant are his references to *Amanita muscaria* chemistry and effects. Allegro had not utilized the *newest* material available. There is no evidence to suggest he ignored it deliberately. There was a huge amount of contradictory information during the period when Allegro wrote *SMC*. No doubt his misunderstandings of these matters came as a result of the confusion and contradiction existent in the publications.

We may discern that Allegro pored over Ramsbottom's book word by word. Allegro found a similar chemical description to Ramsbottom's in Puharich's book. However, Ramsbottom stated that the "chemical structure is not yet ascertained," and Allegro likely (and properly) assumed this was simply due to his book being written before newer publications (such as Puharich, 1959). Ramsbottom connected *Amanita* to the berserkers.

Allegro copied the errors of Dr. Andrija Puharich because Puharich claimed, "The chemical studies with the mushroom confirmed what had already been found in the literature and did not turn up any new evidence." We may therefore understand why Allegro felt safe in using Puharich as a source for the chemical constituents – he was a trained medical professional, a doctor, and former Captain to the US Army Chemical Center at Edgewood, Maryland. He was not just "a man". Puharich had also worked with Wasson, which would make his position more believable. Regardless, Puharich appears to have had ulterior motives by implying that he had reanalyzed the chemicals present in the *A. muscaria*. I've likewise revealed what appears to be an ulterior motive behind Wasson's denigration of Puharich, calling him dismissively "a man". This point casts serious doubt on Wasson's integrity.

The Ethnopharmacologic Search for Psychoactive Drugs, 1967, which Allegro clearly used as a reference for Wasson, also contains all of the detailed and proper chemical analysis of *A. muscaria*. Wasson's essay, cited by Allegro, is at pgs. 405–414. The *A. muscaria* chemical composition essays by Brekhman and Sam, Eugster, and Waser that were *not* used by Allegro directly follow (pg. 415–439). Allegro did not use these three essays, which represented the latest research on the *A. muscaria* chemistry at the time of writing *The Sacred Mushroom and the Cross*, though he had checked four other sources. Did he not have a full copy of this publication – possibly only a photocopy of certain sections? Did he come across this information late in writing *SMC*, too late to rewrite such a large section? Or did Wasson's contradiction of this information in *Soma* simply confuse matters? The answer we may never know. I consulted both the Allegro estate and his associates and none have seen a copy of this publication in the Allegro archives.

Allegro took his descriptions of the fly-agaric's taste from Ramsbottom and Robert Graves, who was a close personal friend of Wasson. Except for the berserker rage cited by the other scholars, it is evident that Allegro acquired the majority of the inferences about the fly-agaric's relation to violence from Graves.

We see that Allegro cited Schultes, *Hallucinogens of Plant Origin*, 1969, but here, too, the chemistry of the Amanita might still be unclear to someone that was not an expert in this specific field of inquiry. Schultes properly described muscimol and ibotenic acid in this publication, but blurs the matter by saying "other as yet uncharacterized principles may take part in the toxicity..." He also repeated his agreement regarding berserker violence after Wasson published extensively against this inference in *Soma*, 1968.

Allegro likely misunderstood the proper usage of tobacco and DMT-based snuffs proposed by Henry Wassen. Allegro's inference to *A. muscaria* snuff is inconclusive and needs further investigation. Allegro overlooked the indigenous Bedouin peoples of Palestine as a possible source for a local culture that appears to have used Ayahuasca analogues and harmala snuffs.

Both Wasson and Allegro found themselves fascinated by a subject which lay outside their professional specialties. Wasson was a financial executive and student of literature; while Allegro was a philologist and expert in Hebrew and Aramaic. Their interest in *Amanita muscaria* and the like took them both deep into the worlds of anthropology, botany, and organic chemistry: far beyond their own spheres of specialization.

Assessing Allegro's motivations and sources, in light of the new evidence presented here with regard to iconography and the holy mushroom of Mt. Athos, will require a major new appraisal of his work. People have dismissed Allegro and his research for many reasons. They've claimed that he was seeking revenge for being treated unfairly over the Dead Sea Scrolls, or just out to make a fast buck. Others claimed that he was a lunatic, or that he'd had a mental breakdown. Yet others have claimed that his research holds no value, that he made up his sources and references, and that there is no truth in his work whatsoever. Their attacks have now been shown to be baseless accusations. Allegro's references with regard to entheogens, for the most part, with mostly minor errors, are valid.

I suggest that Wasson was resentful and jealous toward Allegro for doing what he never had the courage to do—to study mushrooms in Judeo-Christianity. If Allegro was correct, then Wasson's own 1000_{BCE} theory fell into shambles. This seems far more likely than Ruck's proposition that Wasson waffled over the matter for more than 30 years. More likely, Wasson simply did not want to publicly admit that his own work was erroneous.

Thinking of the entire situation in this way, I must ask: Did Wasson have it out for Allegro? Did he want to ruin Allegro for publicly pointing out his own waffling position regarding the 1000_{BCE} theory and the Plaincourault fresco—"rightly or wrongly"? Was Wasson never able to get over the fact that Allegro got the better of him in this one area of his research—Judeo-Christianity? This seems likely, but since his attack in the *TLS* was proactive, we must also consider Wasson's own profit motive—to use the publication of Allegro's book to further advertise his own, as he did in the September 16 letter to the *TLS*.

And why did Wasson send information to an investment firm regarding Allegro's payment? In my opinion, this seems to go far beyond the borders of reasonable ethics, once again placing Wasson's integrity in serious jeopardy.

Wasson's published and public statements and actions make Ruck's position (that Wasson changed his mind regarding the Plaincourault fresco and mushrooms in Christianity) difficult to justify. And if Ruck is correct, then Wasson is proven a hypocrite. Wasson's statements, which are (in most cases) publicly available, and a few letters of his, nearly all contradict Ruck's position. Furthermore, Wasson never apologized to

Allegro, nor did he print a retraction for the inaccurate statements he made. Attempts to communicate ceased: maybe that is how Ruck means that Wasson distanced himself from Allegro (Ruck, *Fungus Redivivus*)? Otherwise, he only made blanket statements against Allegro without thoroughly studying *SMC* first.

Academia needs to learn from the errors of these men. Sometimes sensitivities can arise if people do not have the full confidence which formal training and qualification in a subject tend to create, and even then, as with Panofsky, there is still no guarantee. We need to learn to discern valid information from false assumptions and slanderous claims by taking the time to verify scholars' citations without blanket dismissive or accepting attitudes simply because something challenges or supports orthodox or personal opinions. If we don't learn from this, if we don't learn to think outside the box, outside of orthodoxy, then how will we ever grow?

I have provided sound evidence on which to base further investigation into the proposition that Judeo-Christianity's foundations were based on psychoactive substances after 1000_{BCE}. It has been revealed that Wasson's self-limiting claims are baseless conjectures that appear to stem from his own self interests and wrongful acceptance of the Panofsky interpretation of the Plaincourault fresco.

> ...if even one only of the mushroom references of the cryptic phrases of the New Testament text were correct, then a new element has to be reckoned with in the nature and origin of the Christian religion.
> ~ John Allegro

> Now that the context has been established, even without the evidence of John Allegro, the same conclusion can be drawn. And he was, in fact, right about a mushroom ~~cult~~ in Judeo-Christianity. [Strikethrough added]
> ~ Carl Ruck, *Fungus Redivivus*

The time has come for the acceptance and incorporation of John M. Allegro's valid research into the fields of both biblical theology and entheobotany. His insights and contributions, and those of other scholars studying entheogens in Christianity after him, are certain to move the study of Judeo-Christianity and its origins forward—far beyond his pioneering theories—for decades to come. Let us no longer be restrained by outmoded, prejudiced beliefs.

Appendix—The Allegro-Wasson Controversy

By Jack Herer

The *Amanita muscaria* craze of the 1960s sparked the interest of several researchers interested in this particular mushroom around the world. Most of those who went on to publish papers or write books took sides in the great debate about whether or not there was an historic Jesus Christ, an actual living, walking, talking being, or not. Allegro stated clearly that Jesus was a mushroom and not a walking talking humanoid but the mushroom, period. Gordon Wasson wrote about Hinduism and claimed that Soma, the Hindu plant god, was the *Amanita muscaria* mushroom and not a walking talking humanoid. This concept was easier for some Vedic scholars because Soma was not thought to be a walking, talking god-Man but a mythological character sometimes represented as a plant, the Sun, the Moon etc.

Allegro wrote about the Abrahamic religions being branches evolved from mushroom cults of the old world. The three big religions that developed from the story of Abraham are Judaism, Christianity and Islam (historically created in that order). John Allegro exposes all three of these Abrahamic belief systems as religions that worship the mushrooms as gods in the book *The Sacred Mushroom and the Cross*. Wasson wrote about Hinduism being based upon an ancient belief system that believed the mushrooms were gods as well but for some strange reason Wasson could not grasp Allegro's research as validating and being complementary to his own. Instead he stated publicly that he did not agree with Allegro and the following are the results of this error.

I contacted Richard Schultes in 1984 because of an article wherein Schultes and Wasson were quoted as not agreeing with Allegro's book. Richard Schultes was the director of the Harvard Botanical Museum at the time and when I called I was patched right through. I was calling because I had been extensively researching Allegro's findings and was amazed at the vastness of his work. Researching every reference, I spent thousands of hours going through every footnote and Bible passage that Allegro put forward in the book and he knew the material inside out. Even down to interpreting *The Song of Songs (Cant of Cants)* word for word in the original Hebrew, meticulously decoding the secrets of the mushrooms hidden within. I could not understand why Schultes would make such a statement, so I called to ask him personally. When I asked the great ethnobotanist why he was in disagreement with Allegro's thesis he responded that he never said that he disagreed, but that he was not a linguist, philologist or qualified to critique Allegro's book and that his words were more along the lines of "I'm not qualified to agree or disagree with Allegro's findings". However if I wanted to know why Mr. Wasson had said that *he* disagreed, I could give him a call. I did exactly that, only at the time Gordon was not at home but on vacation in Florida.

When I called back and asked Gordon why he had said that he disagreed with John Allegro's findings as presented in *The Sacred Mushroom and the Cross* Wasson's response was that he gave Allegro's book to two of his friends, one a Jewish Rabbi and the other a Monsignor in the Catholic Church. He said both of them returned the books and assured him that "there was not one single word of truth in the book, whatsoever". I told Gordon the same thing I had expressed to Richard Schultes; "The work is impeccable, Allegro is a scholar of the highest magnitude and I have spent the last six months from eight to fifteen hours a day researching his references and findings; he has not made a mistake, excepting one or two minor errors". Wasson responded that he gave the books to his friends because he trusted their opinions and did not have the time to research it thoroughly himself.

This was an error with repercussions that stretched across time and space, from scholars to casual researchers around the globe. The bottom line is these friends of Wasson's blew Allegro off because they were unable to understand the subject matter, either that or were sworn to secrecy never to reveal the mushroom/god connection. Neither the Rabbi nor the Monsignor could have possibly known the trouble they would cause by their ignorance or secrecy. The simple fact of the mushrooms being "The God of The Universe" to an average Joe in either of these two religions is likely to be too much to even consider, at least back in the 1960s, before anything about this subject had seen the light of day at all. But to reject the thesis off hand without even looking at it, because anyone who looked at it could not possibly say "there was not one single word of truth in the book, whatsoever" (unless they were complete morons or trying overly hard to hide something desperately) is a scholarly crime as serious as the theft of intellectual property (plagiarism). Yet strange motivations have always been at the roots of the Pharmacratic Inquisition and the witch-hunts or crusades.

Many different theories began to spread regarding who Jesus was or was not. This is a debate that has been ongoing for centuries but now there were some new candidates for the personage. Most people with a Christian background that found out about the mushroom rejected Allegro on the basis of the denial of an historic Christ but accepted that the mushroom played some type of role. The Jewish community rejected Allegro on the grounds of him claiming Yahweh was a mushroom but many began to see new meanings in the Jewish texts, and the mystical Kabala was exposed to the uninitiated. There are also Christians who know about the mushroom with a Wassonian slant and believe in a historic Jesus who was revealing the deepest secrets of God by giving the mushrooms to his disciples. The attacks against Allegro were merciless and they are explained in his book *The End of a Road*. The strangest thing is the way people and even psychonautical authors treat Allegro with vitriol and disrespect, while ripping off his material without giving him the proper credit left and right. From books to articles and magazines Allegro's research can be found under the guise of new discoveries presumptuously exploited by unscrupulous authors.

~ Jack Herer

References

- Acharya S., *The Christ Conspiracy* – AUP, 1999, ISBN: 0-932813-74-7
- Allegro, John, *Physician, Heal Thyself...* – Prometheus, 1985, ISBN: 0-87975-241-6
- Allegro, John, *The Dead Sea Scrolls and the Christian Myth* – Prometheus Book, 1992, ISBN: 0-87975-757-4
- Allegro, John, *Lost Gods* – Michael Joseph, 1977, ISBN: 071811633X
- Allegro, John, *The Chosen People* – Doubleday, 1971
- Allegro, John, *The End of a Road* - MacGibbon and Kee, Ltd., 1970
- Allegro, John, "The Sacred Mushroom" Response to Wasson - *Times Literary Supplement*, written 31 August, pub. 11 September, 1970
- Allegro, John, *The Sacred Mushroom & the Cross* – Doubleday, 1970, ISBN: 0340128755
- Allegro, John, "The Sacred Mushroom and the Cross" (David York, introduction: "Christ and the Sacred Mushroom" February 15, 1970 no. 357), in the *Sunday Mirror (London)*. Serialized April 5, 1970 – April 26, 1970. Transcribed at http://johnallegro.org/Allegro-SundayMirror.htm
- Allegro, John, *The Mystery of the Dead Sea Scrolls Revealed* – Gramercy, 1981, ISBN: 0-517-336456. First published as *The Dead Sea Scrolls* – Penguin, 1956
- Anderson, Godfrey, Scrolls Scholar Slaps at Biblical Cornerstones – John Allegro – *The Fresno Bee*, Fresno California, October 14, 1967
- Brekhman, I. I. and Sam, Y. A., "Ethnopharmacological Investigation of Some Psychoactive Drugs Used by Siberian and Far-Eastern Minor Nationalties [sic] of U.S.S.R." in *Ethnopharmalogic Search for Psychoactive Drugs,* ed. Efron, D., (USPHS Publication No. 1654) Washington DC, 1967, ISBN: 0890040478
- Brown, Judith Anne, Personal correspondence with Jan Irvin, March 25, 2006
- Brown, Judith Anne, *John Marco Allegro The Maverick of the Dead Sea Scrolls* – Wm. B. Eerdmans Publishing Company, 2005, ISBN: 0802828493
- Celdrán, José & Ruck, Carl. Daturas for the Virgin – *Entheos* Vol. 1 No. 2, 2002
- Eugster, Conrad H., "Isolation, Structure and Syntheses of Central-Active Compounds from Amanita Muscaria (L. ex Fr.) Hooker" in *Ethnopharmalogic Search for Psychoactive Drugs,* ed. Efron, D., (USPHS Publication No. 1654) Washington DC, 1967, ISBN: 0890040478

- Forte, Robert, (Editor). *Entheogens and the Future of Religion*, 2000, ISBN: 1889725048
- Furst, Peter T., *Hallucinogens and Culture* – Chandler & Sharp, 1976, ISBN: 0-88316-517-1
- Goldblatt, Harvey. Notes on the Text of Ivan Vysenskyj's *Epistle to the Renegade Bishops* in *Harvard Ukrainian Studies*, Vol. XVIII Num. 1/2 June 1994, ed. by Michael S. Flier – Ukrainian Research Institute of Harvard University, © 1996, ISSN: 0363-5570
- http://www.huri.harvard.edu/pdf/hus_volumes/vXVIII_n1_2_june1994.pdf
- Graves, Robert, *The Greeks Myths*, vol. 1 & 2 – Penguin, 1972, ISBN: 014020508X
- Graves, Robert, *The White Goddess* – expanded and revised, Farrar, Straus and Giroux, 1966, ISBN: 374.5.0493.8
- Graves, Robert, *Food for Centaurs* – Doubleday, 1960
- Griffiths, R.R. et al. Mystical-type experiences occasioned by psilocybin mediate the attribution of personal meaning and spiritual significance 14 months later – *Journal of Psychopharmacology*, July 1, 2008, doi:10.1177/0269881108094300
- Griffiths, R.R. et al, *Psilocybin can occasion mystical-type experiences having substantial and sustained personal meaning and spiritual significance* – Johns Hopkins University, May 2006 DOI 10.1007/s00213-006-0457-5
- Herer, Jack et al, *The Most High* – unpublished, 2004
- Herer, Jack, *The Emperor Wears No Clothes: The Authoritative Historical Record of Cannabis and the Conspiracy Against Marijuana*, 11th edition – Ah-Ha Publishing, 2000, ISBN: 1-878125-02-8
- Hoffman, Michael & Irvin, Jan. "Wasson and Allegro on the Tree of Knowledge as Amanita," *Journal of Higher Criticism*, ed. Robert Price, online at: http://www.egodeath.com/WassonEdenTree.htm
- Hoffman, Mark, Correspondences with Michael Hoffman and Jan Irvin, August 28, 2007
- Irvin, Jan & Rutajit, Andrew, *Astrotheology & Shamanism* – The Book Tree, 2006, ISBN: 1-58509-107-3
- Jochelson, W., "The Yukaghir and Yukaghirized Tungus" in *Jesup N. Pacific Expedition Series vol. IX*: (American Museum of Natural History), N.Y., 1926
- Jochelson, W., "Religion and myths of the Koryak" in *Jesup North Pacific Expedition VI, I*
- Letcher, Andy, Personal correspondence to Jan Irvin, April 2, 2007

- Letcher, Andy, *Shroom – A Cultural History of the Magic Mushroom* – HarperCollins, 2007, ISBN: 9780060828288
- Levenda, Peter, *Sinister Forces* Book One – Trineday, 2005, ISBN: 0975290622
- Lewis, Mark, Dir/Prod., "Day of the Zulu," in the PBS T.V. series *Secrets of the Dead,* 2001
- Lipp, Frank J., "Mixe Concepts and Uses of Entheogenic Mushrooms" in *Sacred Mushroom Seeker* ed. by Thomas J. Riedlinger - Park Street Press, 1997, ISBN: 0-89281-338-5
- Merkur, Dan, *The Mystery of Manna* – Park Street Press, 2000, ISBN: 0-89281-772-0
- Müller-Ebeling, Rätsch, Storl, *Witchcraft Medicine: Healing Arts, Shamanic Practices, and Forbidden Plants* – Inner Traditions, 2003, ISBN: 089281971-5
- Ott, Jonathan, Personal correspondence to Jan Irvin, April 30, 2008
- Ott, Jonathan, *Pharmacotheon: Entheogenic drugs, their plant sources and history* 2nd edition – Natural Products Company, 1996, ISBN: 0-9614234-9-8
- Pilch, John, Personal correspondence to Jan Irvin, July 22, 2003
- Pliny the Elder, *The Natural History* (eds. John Bostock, M.D., F.R.S., H.T. Riley, Esq., B.A.) http://www.perseus.tufts.edu/
- Puharich, Andrija, *The Sacred Mushroom: Key to the Door of Eternity* - Doubleday, 1959
- Ramsbottom, John, *Mushrooms & Toadstools: A Study of the Activities of Fungi,* 1st edition – Collins, 1953
- Ramsbottom, John, *Mushrooms & Toadstools: A Study of the Activities of Fungi,* 2nd edition – Collins, 1954
- Rätsch, Christian, *The Encyclopedia of Psychoactive Plants* – Inner Traditions, 2005, ISBN: 089281978-2
- Riedlinger, Thomas J., *Sacred Mushroom Seeker* – Park Street Press, 1997, ISBN: 0-89281-338-5
- Ruck, Carl et al, *The Hidden World: Survival of Pagan Shamanic Themes in European Fairytales* – Carolina Academic Press, 2007, ISBN-10: 1594601445
- Ruck, Carl; Staples, Danny; Celdrán, José., *Melusina of Plaincourault* - 2005
- Ruck, Carl and Staples, Danny., *Heretical Visionary Sacraments* – Peter Webster, 2004
- Ruck, Hoffman, Staples, "Conjuring Eden," *Entheos: The Journal of Psychedelic Spirituality*, Vol. 1, No. 1, 2001

- Ruck, Carl, *Fungus Redivivus: New Light on the Mushroom Controversy* – unpublished
- Rush, John, *Failed God, Fractured Myth in a Fragile World* – North Atlantic Books, 2008, ISBN: 978-1-58394-274-1
- Sajdi, Rami, private emails to Jan Irvin, Sept. 2007
- Sajdi, Rami, *Desert Land* – www.acacialand.com, 1997
- Samorini, G., "'Mushroom-Trees' in Christian Art", *Eleusis* ns 1, 1998, pg. 87–108
- Schultes, R. E., ed. *"Ethnobotany: The Evolution of a Discipline"* – Dioscorides Press, 1995
- Schultes, R. E., "Hallucinogens of Plant Origin" in *Science* Vol. 163, No. 3864, 17 Jan. 1969
- Shanon, Benny, "Biblical Entheogens: a Speculative Hypothesis" in *Time and Mind* Vol. 1, Issue 1, March 2008, pp. 51–74
- Toporov, Vladimir Nikolaevic. "On the Semiotics of Mythological Conceptions about Mushrooms": 295-357. In *Semiotica*, vol 53, n° 4 (1985). Translated from the Russian by Stephen Rudy
- Wahba, S.K. & Elkheir, Y.M., "Dimethyltryptamine from the leaves of certain Acacia species of northern Sudan" – *Lloydia* 38, 176–177, 1975
- Waser, P.G., "The Pharmacology of Amanita Muscaria" in *Ethnopharmalogic Search for Psychoactive Drugs*, ed. Efron, D., (USPHS Publication No. 1654) Washington DC, 1967 , ISBN: 0890040478
- Wassen, H., "Anthropological Survey of the Use of South American Snuffs" in *Ethnopharmalogic Search for Psychoactive Drugs,* ed. Efron, D., (USPHS Publication No. 1654) Washington DC, 1967, ISBN: 0890040478
- Wasson, R.G., Private letter to Mr. Alan Hamilton, 6 July 1985
- Wasson, Kramrisch, Ott, Ruck, *Persephone's Quest: Entheogens and the Origins of Religion* – Yale University Press, 1986, ISBN: 0-300-05266-9
- Wasson, R.G., "The Sacred Mushroom" Response to John Allegro – *Times Literary Supplement*, written 16 September, pub. 25 September, 1970
- Wasson, R.G., Private letter to Arthur Crook, editor of the *Times Literary Supplement*, 16 September, 1970
- Wasson, R.G., Private letter to John Allegro, 14 September 1970
- Wasson, R.G., "The Sacred Mushroom" Public letter to John Allegro – *Times Literary Supplement*, pub. 21 August 1970

- Wasson, R.G., *Soma: Divine Mushroom of Immortality* – Harcourt Brace Jovanovich, Inc., 1968
- Wasson, R.G., "Fly Agaric and Man" in *Ethnopharmalogic Search for Psychoactive Drugs,* ed. Efron, D., (USPHS Publication No. 1654) Washington DC (1967), ISBN: 0890040478
- Wasson, V.P & R.G., *Mushrooms, Russia and History* – Pantheon Books, 1957
- Wasson, R.G., "Seeking the Magic Mushroom" in *LIFE Magazine,* May 13, 1957
- Wilson, Peter Lamborn, *Ploughing the Clouds: The Search for the Irish Soma* – City Lights, 1999, ISBN: 0-87286-326-3

Index

A

Acharya S
  Murdock, D. M. 3
Adam 117
Adam and Eve 117
Allegro
  John 2, 3, 4, 5, 6, 8, 9, 11, 12, 13, 14,
      15, 16, 17, 18, 19, 20, 22, 23, 24,
      25, 26, 28, 29, 30, 31, 41, 43, 54,
      55, 56, 57, 58, 59, 65, 66, 68, 72,
      73, 76, 77, 79, 80, 81, 82, 85, 88,
      89, 91, 92, 94, 95, 99, 100, 101,
      102, 103, 105, 107, 148, 150,
      154, 155, 156, 157, 158, 159,
      160
Amanita
  muscaria 2, 3, 8, 10, 12, 13, 27, 33,
      39, 40, 41, 43, 44, 50, 54, 55,
      57, 58, 61, 64, 65, 66, 68, 69,
      70, 71, 72, 74, 75, 76, 87, 92,
      94, 99, 100, 101, 102, 107, 112,
      115, 116, 117, 121, 123, 136,
      139, 140, 143, 155, 156, 157,
      161
  fly-agaric 6, 15, 17, 19, 20, 21, 22,
      23, 25, 26, 30, 36, 40, 41, 42,
      43, 44, 47, 52, 53, 56, 57, 65,
      76, 81, 89, 96, 97, 98, 99, 139,
      156
  pantherina 33, 44, 45, 55
Ayahuasca analogues 68, 157

B

Bedouin 68, 157
Brekhman and Sam 54, 156

C

caduceus 117
Chukchee 42, 43
CIA 24
Crook
  Arthur 6, 17, 18, 79

D

Dead Sea Scrolls 25, 27, 29, 83, 85, 157
DMT 68, 157

E

entheogen 4, 102, 104
Eugster
  Conrad 20, 54, 55, 156

F

Forte
  Robert 80, 84, 85, 89, 91, 92, 94, 101,
      102, 154
Furst
  Dr. Peter T. 38

G

Garden of Eden 116, 117
Genesis 1, 4, 23, 80, 87, 97, 99, 100,
      101, 102
Goldblatt
  Professor Harvey 149
González-Celdrán
  José 103, 104

Graves
  Robert 27, 31, 41, 56, 59, 60, 61, 64,
    65, 66, 72, 73, 77, 155, 156, 157

H

Hamilton
  Mr. Alan 83, 94, 102, 154
Harvard
  Botanical Museum 161
Herer
  Jack 12, 13, 83, 102, 103, 154, 161,
    163
Hoffman
  Mark 79, 80, 84, 101, 154
  Michael 23, 100, 102
Hofmann
  Dr. Albert 31, 32, 38, 49, 93
holy mushroom
  the 149, 150, 157

I

Irvin
  Jan R. 27, 83, 91, 104, 105

J

Jesus 116
Jochelson
  W. 31, 43, 44

K

Kamchatka 36, 61
Knights of Malta 104
Koryak 36, 37, 42, 43, 44, 47, 50, 75

L

Letcher
  Dr. Andy 2, 93, 94
Levenda
  Peter 24
Lewis
  Mark 54, 66, 68

M

Mazatec Indians 93
Merkur
  Dr. Dan 2
MK-ULTRA 24

O

Opium 117
Ott
  Jonathan 2, 89, 90, 105

P

Panofsky
  Dr. Erwin 1, 3, 8, 9, 13, 15, 23, 25, 26,
    29, 58, 95, 103, 154, 159
Partington
  Anna 27, 28
Pilch
  Dr. John 2, 4
Plaincourault fresco 1, 2, 3, 4, 5, 8, 12,
    13, 14, 16, 19, 22, 23, 29, 39, 41,
    73, 79, 81, 92, 94, 96, 99, 107,
    108, 148, 154, 158, 159
Pliny 44, 46, 47, 61, 67
Price
  Dr. Robert 3, 4, 105
Psilocybe 49, 57, 59, 65, 107, 114, 116,
    117, 119, 143, 152

Psilocybin 32, 93, 152
Puharich
    Andrija 24, 41, 56, 68, 69, 71, 72, 73,
        74, 77, 92, 155, 156

R

Ramsbottom
    Dr. John 13, 14, 15, 16, 17, 18, 27, 31,
        32, 33, 34, 36, 39, 40, 41, 42, 43,
        44, 45, 47, 48, 55, 56, 58, 59, 72,
        73, 81, 82, 83, 95, 102, 154, 155,
        156
Renegade Bishops
    The Epistle to the 149
Rätsch
    Dr. Christian 57, 80
Ruck
    Professor Carl A.P. 1, 3, 26, 28, 29,
        68, 79, 80, 81, 82, 84, 91, 92, 93,
        94, 95, 100, 101, 103, 104, 105,
        107, 154, 158, 159

S

Sabina
    Maria 93
Samorini
    Giorgio 1, 26, 29, 81, 107, 154
Schultes
    Dr. Richard Evans 31, 41, 50, 56, 58,
        73, 74, 75, 76, 157
serpent 116, 117
SMC
    The Sacred Mushroom and the Cross
        6, 13, 23, 27, 31, 92, 107, 148,
        155, 156, 159
spittle 35, 38
Sunday Mirror
    The 88, 91, 92
Syrian Rue 117

T

TLS
    The Times Literary Supplement 6, 8,
        12, 14, 16, 17, 18, 19, 79, 82, 91,
        94, 95, 100, 154
Toporov
    Vladimir Nikolaevic 29, 101

U

US Army Chemical Center 156
US Federal Reserve 93

W

Waser
    Peter 54, 156
Wassen
    Henry 31, 66, 67, 68, 157
Wasson
    Gordon 1, 2, 4, 5, 6, 7, 9, 11, 12, 13,
        15, 16, 17, 18, 19, 23, 24, 25, 26,
        29, 30, 31, 37, 39, 41, 43, 44, 48,
        49, 50, 54, 56, 58, 59, 61, 63,
        65, 72, 73, 74, 76, 79, 80, 81, 82,
        83, 84, 86, 87, 88, 89, 90, 91, 92,
        93, 94, 95, 98, 99, 100, 101, 102,
        103, 104, 105, 107, 154, 155,
        156, 157, 158, 159, 168
Webster
    Donald C. 90, 91
Wilson
    Peter Lamborn 80

Y

Yukaghir 42, 43, 44

Made in the USA
Charleston, SC
09 February 2010